Good Night, Sweet Dreams, I Love You

NOW GET INTO BED AND GO TO SLEEP!

Also from the Boys Town Press

Help! There's a Toddler in the House!

Common Sense Parenting®, 4th Edition

Common Sense Parenting® of Toddlers and Preschoolers

Common Sense Parenting® DVD Series

   Building Relationships

   Teaching Children Self-Control

   Preventing Problem Behavior

   Correcting Misbehavior

   Teaching Kids to Make Good Decisions

   Helping Kids Succeed in School

La Crianza Práctica de los Niños Pequeños

Show Me Your Mad Face

Great Days Ahead: Parenting Children Who Have
   ADHD with Hope and Confidence

Raising Children without Losing Your Voice or Your Mind (DVD)

Adolescence and Other Temporary Mental Disorders (DVD)

No Room for Bullies

Competing with Character

Practical Tools for Foster Parents

La Crianza Práctica de los Hijos

*For students in Grades K-6, see the back of this book for a list of
popular children's titles that highlight important social skills.*

**For a Boys Town Press catalog, call 1-800-282-6657
or visit our website: BoysTownPress.org**

BOYS TOWN NATIONAL HOTLINE®
1-800-448-3000

A crisis, resource and referral number for kids and parents

Good Night, Sweet Dreams, I Love You

NOW GET INTO BED AND GO TO SLEEP!

Patrick C. Friman, Ph.D.

x

Boys Town, Nebraska

**Good Night, Sweet Dreams, I Love You
Now Get into Bed and Go to Sleep!**
Published by the Boys Town Press
Father Flanagan's Boys' Home
Boys Town, NE 68010

Copyright © 2005, by Father Flanagan's Boys' Home
ISBN 1-889322-65-2
ISBN 978-1-889322-65-0

 The Boys Town Press is the publishing
division of Boys Town, a national
organization serving youth and families.

Publishers' Cataloging-in-Publication Data

Friman, Patrick C.

Good night, sweet dreams, I love you : now get into bed and go to sleep! /
Patrick C. Friman. -- 1st ed. -- Boys Town, Neb. : Boys Town Press, 2005.

p. ; cm.

Includes bibliographical references.

ISBN 13: 978-1-889322-65-0

1. Bedtime. 2. Children--Sleep. 3. Sleep disorders in children. 4.
Discipline of children. 5. Child rearing. I. Title.

HQ784.B43 F75 2005
649/.1--dc22   0502

10 9 8 7 6 5 4

TABLE OF CONTENTS

Chapter 1

The Basics of Sleep

"To sleep: perchance to dream..."
- William Shakespeare

We all wish our children sweet dreams. But before this can happen, they have to go to bed and fall asleep! And for many parents, that is when the nightmares begin. There are few things more frustrating than vainly attempting, night after night, to get unwilling children to go to bed, stay in bed, and eventually go to sleep. Children with bedtime problems are not the only ones at risk for lost sleep. Parents are too, especially when their kids consistently will not or cannot learn to go to bed and sleep through the night. When this happens, parents often resort to desperate measures.

An old and popular commercial warned, "It's not nice to mess with Mother Nature." I have a warning that is even more ominous: "It's not nice to mess with Mother Nature, especially when she has not had enough sleep." To prevent sleep loss for the kids and themselves, some parents will do almost anything – beg or bargain, coax or coddle, yell at or threaten their child, embargo, kidnap or even destroy objects their child treasures, and do even worse things that I won't get into here – to get a decent night's sleep.

As parents and so-called parenting experts have lamented for years, children do not arrive on this earth with an instruction booklet attached to their toes, or anywhere else. (When God's performance evaluation is done, this should probably be brought up.) I bought a kitchen knife recently and it came with two pages of instructions. (Apparently kitchen knives are more complicated than most of us have been led to believe.) Still, I believe it is safe to say that even the easiest of children are vastly more complicated than a kitchen knife (and possibly more dangerous). And if instructions were available for kids, a large section would surely be devoted to information on how to get them to go to bed, stay in bed, and go to sleep.

Humans have some very basic needs. Food and water are at the top of the list. I suspect that if parents across the world were to vote for a No.

3, a good night's sleep would win hands down
(or hands up, depending on how the votes are
counted). Getting enough sleep (or not getting
enough sleep) can greatly affect how a family functions and how family members get along. When
people get proper rest, they are better equipped
to handle life on life's terms (and it does not
take very many trips around the sun to realize
how tough those terms are). Sleep makes people
more energetic and better able to deal with daily
events in a positive way. On the other hand, lack
of sleep makes most people grouchy or cranky
and prone to frustration, irritation, and anger.
Relationships become strained and suffer, and it
can be a struggle just to make it to the end of the
day without catfights, hissy fits, or extended con-
temptuous contemplations of one's betters and
"worsers." Nature's design has made the bosom of
one's family the safest place for family members
to be, but if a few members are suffering from lack
of sleep, especially those at the top of the family's
organizational chart, the rest of the family might
be safer in some war-torn country. Said more
seriously and soberly, lack of sleep, especially
in parents, can lead to a toxic state in which the

whole family – children and parents alike – experiences harmful physical and emotional effects.

Without belaboring the point, let's just say that the value of a good night's sleep is hard to overestimate. Unfortunately, as many as 25 to 30 percent of children in this country experience some kind of problem that interferes with them getting good sleep. Most of these problems are related to children going to bed, staying in bed, and going to sleep, which is the focus of this book. These children are almost certainly causing sleep problems for their parents. (There are more serious sleep-related disorders; we will mention some of them later in the book.)

There are many – way too many – children and parents facing the world daily with too little sleep because of bedtime problems. But help is at hand, at least for you. A bold claim to be sure, but one I intend to make good on. You can learn better ways to make bedtime a relaxed, uneventful, and enjoyable part of the day. In fact, most children can and *will* go to bed without much fuss and hassle if parents can create the right conditions and follow through on them properly and consistently. You can help your children overcome sleep problems so that everyone in the family is rested and alert, and your children are able to grow and learn with charm and humor. Sounds easy, doesn't it? Well, okay, that may be a bit of false advertising. It may not be easy in every case, and in some cases it will be very difficult, but it is something that can be achieved and doing so will make virtually everything else much easier.

You want what's best for your children, even if they did keep you up half the night last night and, right now, you might not know what's best if it bit you on the neck. This little book can help you give them what's best in the area of sleep by offering some tried-and-true ways to identify and solve sleep problems with children. Think of what is presented in the following pages as a "guide" to children's bedtime and sleep. In that sense, it is not unlike a treasure map ("Follow these steps, matey, and you'll find the treasure.") This guide will describe how to build and promote healthy bedtime habits, implement practical and easy-to-use strategies to help you deal with sleep problems for kids of all ages, and discuss other special issues about kids' sleep. But best of all, these strategies work and work well. They have been used with thousands of children in our clinic at Boys Town, other clinics across the country, and in numerous research studies. I am confident they will work for you, too.

The book is easy to read and easy to use, so you'll get the most out of it. There are eleven chapters. I begin with information on why children need a lot of sleep. Then I discuss at length how children learn new skills or ways of doing things. How children learn is pretty central to, well, teaching them. If they are having bedtime problems, they will need to learn some new stuff. So the chapter on learning is very important, and it figures prominently throughout the chapters that follow. Those chapters address bedtime rituals, sleep problems, and effective ways to approach them for children in a specific age group – infants, toddlers, preschoolers, elementary school kids, and middle school or high school youngsters. Chapter 10 briefly discusses some special bedtime and sleep situations that parents might encounter with their children.

No matter how old your child is, I hope you read the entire book; while the focus is on solving sleep problems, the chapters hold many suggestions and advice for a range of child and parenting issues.

Sleep Problems and Sleep Disorders

Before I go any further, let's talk a bit about the difference between "sleep problems" and "sleep disorders." Most parents, if properly educated and motivated, can help children work through sleep problems. Fundamentally, child sleep problems are actually behavior problems that involve the three target behaviors I mentioned earlier: going to bed, staying in bed, and going to sleep. Children who have problems with these three behaviors almost always have skill deficits. Quite simply, they have not yet learned what they are supposed to do at bedtime and how to do it. So in that sense, bedtime problems involve "won't'" or "don't know how" types of problems. But children can experience many other types of sleep-related difficulties, and most professionals refer to these as "sleep disorders" rather than "sleep problems." (To be technically correct, they are called either *parasomnias* or *dysomnias*, but I don't want to drag any more Greek- or Latin-based gobbledygook into this book than I have to.) Sleep disorders do not involve "won't" or "don't know how" type of problems; they involve "can't" types of problems. Children who wet the bed at night, for example, cannot stop even if they really, really want to, which virtually all of them want to do. These situations typically cannot be addressed by the kinds of advice I offer here without additional advice from a professional. There are too many of these "can't" problems to discuss here but I do mention a few in Chapter 10. The trick is to determine when a sleep problem is a problem and when it is a disorder. I won't go too deeply into that area but I will provide some helpful advice.

There are many other books available on children's sleep problems, and almost all of them are more technical than this one. Most involve comprehensive sections on the difference between sleep problems and sleep disorders. I will list a few of the books I would recommend for parents later, but there are two that I particularly like: *Solve Your Child's Sleep Problems* (Fireside Books, 1985), by Dr. Richard Ferber, and *Sleeping Through the Night* (Quill Harper Resource, 1997), by Dr. Jodi Mindell. Dr. Mindell's book contains a helpful list of symptoms that suggest whether a child's bedtime or sleep troubles may be a disorder. In summary, the list calls on parents to watch for:

- Any problems with breathing, including snoring, noisy breathing, mouth breathing, or choking.
- Excessive movement while sleeping, especially leg or whole body movement.
- Excessive sweating.
- Confusion and expressions of terror.
- Sleep walking.

Any of these can be a red flag that indicates the need for professional help. In general, if you have any questions or concerns about your child's sleep troubles, you should discuss them with your primary care physician before using the strategies offered in this book.

Sleep Basics

What do parents need to know about sleep to help their children? Not much really. We all know that sleep is a basic necessity, something every human being needs to be healthy and energetic. *The American Heritage Dictionary* defines sleep as "a natural, periodic state of rest for the mind and body, in which the eyes usually close and consciousness is completely or partially lost, so that there is a decrease in bodily movement and responsiveness to external stimuli." You might ask, "If sleep is supposed to be natural, why don't children just go to sleep when they're supposed to?" I'll try to help you answer that question, and others, in later chapters. And as any parent who has been awakened by a crying child or whose child has suddenly hopped into Mom's and Dad's bed at one o'clock in the morning knows, there has been no "decrease in bodily movement and responsiveness to external stimuli." How to get children to settle down before bedtime so that they are ready to sleep is another area I'll discuss.

It is also important to know that kids at different ages need different amounts of sleep. Obviously, an infant or toddler requires much more sleep than an adolescent. Also, every child is unique. So, even kids who are the same age might need different amounts of sleep to function well throughout the day. The chart to the right gives you a good framework for determining how much total sleep children at various ages typically need to feel rested and alert.

Typical Sleep Requirements in Childhood

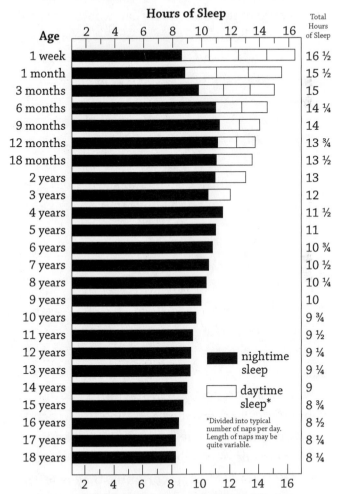

Age	Total Hours of Sleep
1 week	16 ½
1 month	15 ½
3 months	15
6 months	14 ¼
9 months	14
12 months	13 ¾
18 months	13 ½
2 years	13
3 years	12
4 years	11 ½
5 years	11
6 years	10 ¾
7 years	10 ½
8 years	10 ¼
9 years	10
10 years	9 ¾
11 years	9 ½
12 years	9 ¼
13 years	9 ¼
14 years	9
15 years	8 ¾
16 years	8 ½
17 years	8 ¼
18 years	8 ¼

■ nightime sleep

□ daytime sleep*

*Divided into typical number of naps per day. Length of naps may be quite variable.

Obviously, sleep is a complex human activity, and there is much more to it than what is covered in the basic dictionary definition. But it isn't necessary to understand the intricate physical and psychological functions of sleep to help children overcome sleep problems. Except where it might be necessary to cite significant research results, this book will stick to practical ways you can help your children and yourself. If you would like to learn more about the specifics of sleep, there are many good web sites and books that present and discuss this information in detail.

A Final Thought

If you are tired of being tired because your child won't go to bed and sleep, the only reason you might be reading this book is to solve the problem. But correcting sleep problems with your child is part of a bigger parenting picture. Children who master the skill of staying in bed and going to sleep are learning a routine that is good for them and the whole family. They're learning how to be independent of Mom and Dad, if even for a short time. Most importantly, they're learning how to follow instructions and how to deal with a potentially upsetting situation in a calm manner. These are huge milestones for any child, no matter what his or her age is.

Along those same lines, many of the sleep-problem strategies I will provide involve the same parenting skills used in other Boys Town programs. Praising children when they do something well, teaching them what to do in specific situations before those situations occur, using consequences to either reinforce positive behavior or stop negative behavior, and effectively correcting misbehavior are just a few of the components I will describe and explain. These skills will not only help you tackle sleep issues with your kids but also improve how you parent.

Solving children's sleep problems can sometimes be difficult. It requires patience, understanding, perseverance, and most importantly, a whole lot of love on your part. The strategies I will teach you work only when used within the loving, caring relationship you have with your child.

With Boys Town's help, getting your child to sleep at night shouldn't be something you have to lose sleep over anymore.

CHAPTER 2

Children Need Sleep, and Here's Why

Children and adolescents sleep a lot. As Richard Ferber's sleep chart on page 11 shows, newborns sleep 16 to 18 hours a day and adolescents sleep up to 10 hours a day. But why is that? Is a lot of sleep necessary for children to be healthy and happy? Clearly, the answer is "Yes." Decades of scientific research show that sleep – and lots of it – is a key ingredient for the optimal health and well-being of children during all stages of their childhood. Because sleep is so important, bedtime also becomes an important factor in a family's life.

Children and parents receive many benefits when children get the sleep they need. In this chapter, I'll discuss these five benefits: kids replenish their energy; kids learn to handle distress better; kids learn how to follow instructions; parents become better at using appropriate discipline; and parents get a break.

Kids Replenish Their Energy

Abundant science shows that fatigue can weaken a person's ability to pay and maintain attention, learn, regulate emotions, and maintain self-control. Merely resting can help reduce fatigue, but only sleep lets children "recharge their batteries" with the energy they need to successfully manage a typical day.

From the moment they wake up, children are thrown into a succession of demanding situations. Most, if not all, of these situations require different skills and tasks they have not yet fully developed, and perhaps won't fully develop until they reach adolescence. So, when children do not get enough sleep, the already difficult situation of getting through the morning routine can become a major problem for both children and parents.

For example, let's look at the morning routine on a school day for a young child. The child's first major task of the day is waking up. Even when children have had enough sleep, waking up can still be a challenge. For children, as well as adults, it is far easier to wake up fully when a person likes what is going to happen next. For adults, waking for work is harder than waking for golf, fishing, or other forms of fun. Children are the same way. Waking for school is harder than waking for play or favorite cartoons. So, for the average child, waking up on a weekday is usually the first step toward an event they are not very excited about: school.

Waking children with some prodding may be necessary, even when they are well rested. But if children are not well rested and have not had enough sleep, they face the task of waking for school fatigued, groggy, and short on the energy they need for a successful school day (paying attention, emotional regulation, and self-control skills).

Waking a fatigued child often requires more than a little parental prodding. Many times, the methods needed – or at least the methods used – are unpleasant: yelling, shaking, or pulling the child out of bed. This sets the stage for what can be a less-than-happy morning routine. And, as many parents have experienced, an unpleasant morning routine can create an incredible amount of friction between children and parents. Usually, everyone ends up starting the day upset and unhappy. This is not good for tired children because emotional upsets can lead to attention problems, poor self-control, and poor learning. All this results in an obvious fact: A tired, unhappy child is not at his or her best for a productive day in school.

To set your kids up for having the best day possible, and to avoid some of those more harrowing morning routine conflicts, it's important that you ensure your children get the proper amount of sleep. This involves setting appropriate bedtimes and following a positive bedtime routine.

Kids Learn to Handle Distress Better

Children aren't born with a built-in ability to handle distress. They rely heavily on their parents to eliminate or soften sources of distress, ease any discomfort that comes their way, and provide warmth and love when bad or unsettling things happen. A major task during childhood, however, is to learn how to handle distress without parents always having to step in to make things better.

For children to accomplish this task, parents must gradually withdraw their assistance. Parents also must strategically establish limits. Doing this has many benefits. An obvious one is reducing children's behavioral excesses. By excesses, I mean areas where they go over the line – they talk too much, run too fast, pull too hard, push too vigorously, or generally go too far. Another benefit is that children learn how to increase their tolerance for distress that occurs when limits are placed on their behavior. Limits in and of themselves cause varying degrees of distress for children because children don't want their behavior to be limited. When parents enforce limits, children are required to learn how to cope with and manage this distress.

Now, how does all of this relate to sleep and bedtime? One of the first limits parents must set on child behavior is a sensible bedtime. One widely accepted myth in 20th century parenting was that, if left alone, children would naturally select a healthy sleep schedule and diet. The truth is that, without parental guidance, most children will drink an ocean of soda, eat sweets, ice cream, and chips until they're ready to bust, and stay up well past a sensible bedtime, regardless of when they need to be up in the morning. That's why I believe parents must establish limits in these areas to ensure that children do not undermine their own health. Simply put, raising healthy children means that you must control your children's sleep schedule and diet.

Most children will fight a sleep schedule because they want to stay up as long as they can stay awake. Parents who enforce a sleep schedule cause some distress for their children every night. But, as I said, this allows children to learn how to manage distress and practice it every night. This practice and learning helps children improve how they handle distress in general and gradually helps them to become more self-sufficient.

Kids Learn How to Follow Instructions

Knowing how to understand and follow instructions from adult authority figures is an important skill for all children to learn. As with any skill, mastery of following instructions requires practice – and lots of it! Opportunities for practice come from the many different interactions that initially take place between children and their parents, and that later occur between children and a wide range of other adult authority figures (teachers, adult relatives, etc.). These instructions come in the form of household rules, school (from daycare through secondary school) rules, civic and community rules, and others.

One of the first steps in learning to follow instructions involves "surrendering" to adult authority. Here is a bold news flash: **Children are not born knowing how or being willing to follow instructions.** They have to learn this valuable skill. So unless instructions are aimed at getting them to do what they are currently doing, about to do, or already want to do, most children will not follow them unless they have been specifically trained to do so, no matter where the instructions are delivered or from whom they come. It's actually even worse than that for many children. If they have not been adequately taught to follow instructions, they will do what they want to do regardless of what someone tells them to do. There are a lot of words in the English language for this kind of behavior – willful, stubborn, noncompliant, ornery, and so on. There are some Anglo Saxon expletives that make similar points in more powerful, albeit less socially acceptable, ways. I leave it to you to think of your own. However, I prefer to think of such behavior as evidence that a child lacks instructional control skills and needs training.

So, how is learning to follow instructions related to sleep and bedtime problems? Simple. Just like adults, most children want to stay up late. They lack the judgment to understand that doing this will create problems in the morning. Thus, to ensure that your children obtain the proper amount of rest, you must establish a reasonable bedtime for them. You can start by consulting the chart on page 11 that shows how much sleep children need at various ages, and determine a reasonable time for them to go to bed. Since the bedtime you set will almost always be earlier than what your children want, you must give specific instructions about when to go to bed and then enforce those instructions when necessary.

Following instructions is actually a very difficult skill for children to learn. In fact, it's not always an easy skill for adults. Most crimes, troubles on the job, and civic disagreements involve some degree of instructional control problems. People young and old want to do what **they** want to do, not necessarily what someone else wants them to do. Abundant practice is the key to learning this skill.

Following any instruction requires children to interrupt what they are doing and redirect their energy, attention, and general behavior toward what they have been told to do. Complete details about how children learn this and other skills are included in the next chapter. For now, I want to mention one specific component of this process: practice.

Every night when you tell your child to go to bed, your child practices the skill of following instructions. Children want to stay up late and parents want them to go to bed. When you enforce bedtime rules, and your children surrender to parental authority and go to bed, they practice the skill of following instructions. This practice, night after night, greatly contributes to how well children learn this important skill.

Parents Become Better at Using Appropriate Discipline

Early in a child's life, parents discipline their children with a mixture of minor scolding, redirecting them away from inappropriate behavior, time in, and time out. But as children grow older, their behaviors become more complex and parents must develop additional ways to discipline.

No matter what age your child is, you don't want to yell or physically punish him or her, especially for something like not going to bed on time. But it does happen. It's natural for adults to get frustrated and angry with children who aren't complying with bedtime rules. The stress of a long hard day can lead some parents to discipline their children in ways that lead to regret or remorse, harm relationships, and simply don't work.

Parents don't have to discipline in destructive ways. As a parent, you can use bedtime as an opportunity to expand your parenting skills. A sensible bedtime can create an opportunity for you to learn and use new ways to discipline. Let's take a look at three new discipline strategies you can use at bedtime.

- As children grow older, they need less sleep. A sensible bedtime for a 4-year-old may be too early a bedtime for a 6-year-old. In other words, older children might have later bedtimes because they need a little bit less sleep. But rather than automatically making the bedtime later for an older child, parents can use the difference between an existing bedtime and a later one as a reward. This way, parents can have children earn staying up later by meeting certain behavioral standards the parents set down. For example, you could ask your child to consistently follow household rules for a certain amount of time *and* do at least one behavior or task (being particularly nice to a brother and/or sister, helping with household chores, or completing a required task without being asked) that goes beyond that requirement. On days when your child meets the established requirement, he could stay up until the later bedtime. On days when he does not meet the requirement, he would go to bed earlier, nearer his old bedtime. With this new strategy, you would make it clear to the child that regular bedtime is not a punishment; rather, it is the result, or consequence, of perfectly acceptable behavior that didn't rise above routine expectations. To earn the later bedtime, your child must rise above the routine behaviors.

- Another strategy you can use at bedtime is one that classifies as a "punishment" strategy. Here, children who misbehave beyond what you consider to be acceptable or routine are "fined" time, and the time is subtracted from their regular bedtime. One way to do this is to determine the number of half hours between the end of dinner and the regular bedtime and use these half-hour increments as disciplinary units. For example, children whose misbehavior only slightly exceeds household standards could be "fined" one unit and sent to bed a half an hour earlier than their regular bedtime. Children whose misbehavior dramatically exceeds household standards could be sent to bed two or more half hours before their regular bedtime.

- A final example involves using bedtimes that motivate children to do homework. You can require your child to do her regular homework to earn her regular bedtime and have her do extra homework to earn a later bedtime. Conversely, if your child doesn't do her homework, you can send her to bed earlier than her regular bedtime. With this approach, the only way she can stay up later is to do extra homework.

Setting a sensible bedtime when children are young, and then maintaining a consistent time as they get older, sets the stage for powerful new options for disciplining children. These are options and strategies that don't involve yelling or physical punishment – things loving and caring parents don't want to use or do. Learning how to use these strategies at bedtime can enable you to use them in other areas of your child's life where discipline is needed.

Parents Get a Break

The final benefit of setting a sensible bedtime is that you get a breather – time to recharge your batteries, both individually and as a couple. You love your children, treasure the time you spend with them, and think about and miss them when you are away. But even the most loving relationships require occasional separations, and the parent-child relationship is no exception. In addition, to help maintain the quality of the parents' relationship with each other, parents need to spend time together, away from children, friends, and other family. Setting a sensible bedtime creates a healthy separation between parents and their children, and gives parents time to be together alone to nurture their own relationship.

Summary

There are many benefits to establishing a sensible bedtime for children; some are common sense and some are technical. I have emphasized the five benefits I feel are the most compelling. Central to all five is the concept of child learning. How children learn, how the laws of learning can be used to maximize parental teaching, and how learning applies to sleep and bedtime are topics discussed in the next chapter.

CHAPTER 3

How Children Learn, and Why It Matters for Sleep

Solving bedtime problems requires that you understand how children learn. Going to bed at a certain time, staying in bed, and going to sleep are all behaviors that parents want their children to know how to do. In order to teach these behaviors, you have to know what motivates kids to want to change old ways of doing things (not going to bed at a certain time, not staying in bed, and not going to sleep). You also have to know how kids "absorb" new behaviors and get good at using them. In this chapter, I'll discuss some of the important elements of learning for children. Later, I'll talk about how you can effectively use them with sleep problems and with other behaviors you'd like to change.

A century of research shows that child learning mostly results from children making a connection between what they did, to what happened before they did it, and finally, to the change that occurs to them or the world around them because of what they did. The bigger this change, the stronger the connection. For example, a dad asks his 8-year-old son to pick up his toys. The child picks up the toys. Dad gives his boy a pat on the back and tells him, "Thanks for doing that so fast. That was great!" The boy likes the fact that Dad praised him for doing a good job. Because of what happened after the boy did his chore, he is more likely to pick up his toys (or follow other instructions) when Dad asks him to do so in the future. The boy has made a connection between what happened before the behavior (Dad's request), the behavior itself (picking up the toys), and the positive result (praise for a job well done). He has **learned** that following Dad's instructions means that something good will happen to him. I call that "something good" a positive consequence.

Consequences

Consequences – both positive and negative ones – are important parts of child learning. A positive consequence can be the addition of something good, like the praise in the previous example. It also can be avoiding or taking away something unpleasant. For example, if the same boy knew that Dad might not let him play with the toys later if he didn't pick them up when asked, the boy would do what Dad asked to avoid losing his toys.

Negative consequences can be adding something a child doesn't like or taking away something a child likes. In our example, Dad could send the boy to his room for not picking up his toys (taking away the boy's freedom for a short time) or have the boy do an extra chore (adding something the boy doesn't particularly like). When you can determine what your child likes and doesn't like, it gives you a list of possible consequences to use when he or she behaves well or misbehaves.

The general rules for using consequences are:

- Add something a child likes (positive reinforcement) or take away something a child doesn't like (negative reinforcement) in order to get him or her to start using a behavior or to use the behavior more often.
- Add something a child doesn't like (punishment) or take away something a child likes

(response cost) in order to get him or her to stop using a behavior or to use it less often. The following chart illustrates these rules.

	Add	**Subtract**
To Increase a Behavior	**Something Pleasant** (Positive Reinforcement)	**Something Unpleasant** (Negative Reinforcement)
To Decrease a Behavior	**Something Unpleasant** (Punishment)	**Something Pleasant** (Response Cost)

Practice

Practicing is another key part of child learning. The more often a child uses a behavior or has an opportunity to use a behavior, the better he or she will get at using it. This is true for children and adults. Think about something you do well. How did you get good at it? It might be playing the piano, woodworking, fixing your car, baking a cake, or playing a sport. First, you learned the best way to do the skill. Then you practiced, sometimes doing the same behaviors over and over until they began to come naturally to you. Kids are the same way. The more often they use a behavior and begin to understand why they use it, the better they get at it. And when the behavior results in something good (a positive consequence), they are likely to keep on doing it.

How often do children need to practice a behavior before they actually "learn" it? That usually depends on the child, the person who is teaching the behavior, and the consequences that are used. As I said earlier, the bigger the change in what happens to a child after he or she does a behavior, the stronger the child's connection to what happened before the behavior, the behavior itself, and the result. Generally, children who make this "strong" connection require fewer repetitions in order to learn and consistently use the behavior. When the connection is not clear, or when children struggle with understanding how the parts fit together, lots of practice might be necessary before the child catches on. That's why when you teach a new skill or behavior, you must clearly explain what you want your child to do, demonstrate it if necessary, and then explain what will happen both if the child uses the behavior or chooses not to use it.

Putting It Together

Let's look at a simple example of how all these parts work in a real-life situation.

Every parent teaches his or her child not to touch fire or something hot. Fire is very dangerous for children. The first time very young children see fire, they are not aware of the danger, but rather, are fascinated by its beauty. If unsupervised, they will often try to touch it. When this happens, they instantly learn a very important lesson; in other words, they make that connection between what they did and the result. This learning results from the presence of fire (what was happening before the child acted), the child touching the fire (the behavior), and the pain and/or a nasty burn that results (the consequence). This consequence involves so much change in the child (from feeling no pain to feeling intense pain) that the child learns in one experience not to touch fire. Typically, this lesson lasts a lifetime; the child is unlikely to deliberately place his or her hand in an open flame again. This is not to say that children who have been burned will not be burned again, but as the saying goes "Once burned, twice shy."

The power of this type of learning is demonstrated when parents who are trying to teach their toddlers to stay away from breakable household objects may tell them that the objects are "hot." A child who has actually touched something hot will often avoid, at least temporarily, going near objects that he or she has been told are hot.

To put a complex process in simple terms, teaching children new behaviors like following a bedtime routine involves clearly describing the behaviors you want to see, setting and following through with consequences for positive or negative behavior, and practicing the desired behaviors.

Resisting and Ignoring

There is an opposite side to the positive teaching and learning that can take place between you and your children. Just as behaviors that are followed by big changes often require less practice in order for a child to learn the behavior, behaviors that are followed by little or no change often require much more practice. As a result, it can take children a lot longer to learn some new behaviors and skills. While teaching children is an ongoing task for parents, both parents and children can get bored and frustrated if they work on the same behavior for a long time. And for parents who want to teach their children better bedtime habits, quicker learning is preferable to a long, drawn-out ordeal.

What causes this type of situation? Usually, it's not what parents are trying to teach but how they are trying to teach it. Parents who rely on nagging, reminding, warning, and threatening their children don't have much long-term success when it comes to teaching appropriate behavior. These approaches usually involve many attempts at trying to get a child to use a behavior, but with few or no consequences. Without consequences, there is little change for the child. And as I have said, big changes (consequences) are what moti-vate children to learn and use new behaviors.

Nagging, reminding, warning, or threaten-ing also can cause children to resist doing what parents want. The more parents try to get children to use a behavior by using these approaches, the more children will resist. After a while, children will start ignoring their parents because they are tired of being badgered, and they know their parents won't follow through with any consequences. As children get better at ignoring, and parents throw up their hands in frustration and stop trying to teach, children learn that ignoring is a good way to get out of doing what their parents want them to do. They also learn that parents will eventually "give up" and leave them alone.

Another type of parent-child interaction also increases the likelihood children will ignore their parents. In this situation, the parent ignores or barely responds to the child when he or she actually uses an appropriate behavior. Since the child sees no consequence – either positive or negative – for using the behavior, there is no motivation for him or her to try to get better at it. If the child also is being nagged, reminded, warned, and threatened by the parent, ignoring becomes even more likely.

In conclusion, many child behavior problems result from parent-child interactions where misbehaving gets the child better results than behaving appropriately.

Negative Rather Than Nothing

So far, I have made two straightforward points: Children learn through changes (consequences) that happen to them as a result of their behavior and through practicing behaviors. Both of these help children make connections between what they do and what happens to them as a result. In general, children behave in ways that produce pleasant outcomes or experiences and help them avoid unpleasant experiences. Unfortunately, it is not always that simple. In some circumstances, and bedtime is a prime example, children will deliberately behave to produce an unpleasant experience. Most times, this happens when children are receiving no response or outcome to their behavior, whether it is good or bad. In other words, they are experiencing "nothing." Children, especially young ones, do not like "nothing." Kids crave attention. They want to be doing something all the time, and usually they want somebody to be watching or doing it with them. They can't stand to be alone, away from parents or others. If kids have a choice between nothing and something, even if it is negative or unpleasant, they will usually choose negative over nothing. This is one major reason why bedtime is often so unpleasant. Faced with being in bed in the dark with nothing to do, your child may prefer to argue, resist, or defy you even if it means that you get angry.

There are many everyday situations where children face the experience of nothing. One of the most common examples is when a parent with young children talks on the phone for a long time. Frequently, children respond by getting upset and misbehaving, and it sometimes puzzles parents. It shouldn't. The most treasured source of external stimulation for young children is usually the parent, and during telephone calls, the parent provides the child little or no attention. In the unlikely event that children behave appropriately during telephone calls (they sit on the couch and look at picture books), the parent may continue to talk on the phone. When children are behaving appropriately, there is no compelling reason for a parent to stop what he or she is doing and pay attention to them. The unpleasant result for children is an extended experience of nothing (at least as far as the parent, as a source of stimulation, is concerned). In other words, good behavior while a parent is on the telephone usually produces nothing for the child. So children make noise, fight, pull on Mom's pant leg, whine, cry, throw toys, and generally have a fit in order to get Mom's attention again. The parent might respond by hanging up, becoming angry, and punishing the child. Despite this quite logical parental reaction to the problem, child misbehavior during telephone calls often continues to increase rather than decrease. That's because, for the child, something – even a parent's anger – is better than nothing. Through misbehavior, the child replaces nothing with something – a response from the parent. From the perspective of child learning, attempts to discipline child misbehavior occurring in the context of nothing are more likely to increase than decrease the misbehavior.

Nothing and Bedtime

The relationship between how children learn and the motivating effects of the experience of nothing sets the stage for most child behavior problems at bedtime. Bedtime signals a time when nothing interesting is going to happen to a child unless he or she resists in some way. For very young children, the mere act of a parent leaving a child's sight at night is often so distressing that the child will burst out crying the second the parent disappears. This leaves the child alone and close to experiencing nothing, which is highly unpleasant.

Children quickly learn that crying usually brings the parent back, turning the experience of nothing into seeing and being with the parent. It is not surprising that the earliest and most common bedtime behavior problem is crying out from the bedroom.

For children up to six months old, crying out from the bedroom is a normal behavior for that developmental level. Parents may not like it, but it is acceptable. For that reason, you should not try to teach children six months or younger to go to sleep on their own. After that age, however, let the teaching begin! I'm not saying it's wrong to wait until a child is a year or even 18 months old, but it only puts off the training that must take place if a child is to learn bedtime and sleep skills. And the longer you wait to teach your child to sleep on his or her own, the more difficult that teaching will be.

As I said earlier, children quickly learn that if they cry when the parent goes out of sight at bedtime, the parent will return. Because parents do consistently respond to crying, out of necessity, when their child is younger than six months old, most parents are faced with this recurring behavior as their child grows. If the connection the child has learned is not broken sometime between six months and one year, the child's bedtime behavior will eventually worsen and lead to calling out and coming out from the bedroom.

Summary

Helping your children learn new behaviors is not always easy. Teaching your child new behaviors and skills can take time, and you must be patient. But understanding the basics of child learning – that consequences and practice help children make the connection between their behaviors and the changes they experience as a result of what they do – gives you a big advantage in every area of parenting. The importance of this understanding will become clearer as I discuss strategies for developing new bedtime behaviors.

In the next chapter, I will begin to talk about strategies for setting bedtime routines that work.

Chapter 4

The Pre-Bedtime Ritual

The first big step in solving bedtime problems is developing a nurturing pre-bedtime ritual. This step seems to come naturally to parents when children are younger, but it is still important as children get older. When children go to bed, they are in a sense going on a long journey alone. They need certain "sleep skills" if they are to eventually accomplish the task of sleeping alone.

For most children, time spent alone at any other time during the day will not come close to the amount of time they spend alone in bed. For some children, bedtime is stressful and frightening. So even though it happens every night and is as routine as waking up in the morning, a young child who is going to bed alone should receive a big sendoff from loved ones. Much later, when children are preteens or teens, the nightly sendoff ritual may be winnowed to a hug and a kiss. But when kids are small, and the prospect of the journey is still new and more challenging, much more is needed. It is this sincere, significant sendoff that reassures, calms, and prepares the child for the night ahead.

The best way I can describe the sentiment that should go with an appropriate pre-bedtime ritual is to use the phrase "Farewell, my love." Why is that, you may wonder? Let's start with "farewell." Saying "Good night" to children is, in essence, saying "farewell" for an entire night, perhaps as long as 10 hours. This is the longest period of time they will ever spend away from you, the rest of the family, their teachers, their friends, and everyone else. So in a very real sense, you are saying "farewell" to an extremely important person in your life – your child. This brings us to the second part of the message – "my love." The farewell you give your children at night should be one of love. You are saying farewell to someone you love very, very much and someone who loves you very, very much. You are saying farewell because you won't see your child again for a long time and you are saying it in a loving way because love is the prevailing message. Children should go to bed experiencing being loved, and as night continues, that feeling should linger in the air.

The reason I stress love so much here is that the experience of being loved – of being part of something, of being very, very important to someone, of being thought of and thought of well – makes any difficult journey easier. The thought that someone is thinking of us, looking out for us, and wishing us well emboldens us to take new steps in life, to face danger, to face the unknown. A child going to bed has to face a long period of time where he or she will be alone in the dark. Fear of the dark and what might happen in it is the most prevalent child fear. And children are not the only ones who are afraid of the dark. Most adults, if they were honest, would acknowledge that they sometimes, and perhaps often, awake, afraid in the dark. This potential for fear at night is another reason I emphasize the importance of making sure that children feel loved as they begin their journey through the night alone in bed.

Do's and Don'ts

There are many guidelines for establishing a pre-bedtime ritual. Most of them involve common sense rather than anything scientific. The remainder of this chapter will describe some important do's and don'ts.

Winding Down

An important element of the pre-bedtime ritual involves tempo. Generally, children spend their day working themselves up, getting themselves going, revving their motors, gunning their engines, and putting the pedal to the metal. This is all well and good, and it's why children have more fun than adults. However, as bedtime nears, parents should help their children reduce the revs, gear down, slow their engines, and take their feet off the gas pedal. In other words, parents need to "wind down" children so they are prepared for slumber. Giving your child a bath or having him or her take a bath (depending on the child's age) just before the pre-bedtime ritual begins is an excellent way to do this. Spending time soaking in warm water is relaxing, and it can have a calming effect on a child. A bath is not a must before bedtime, but since it is an important part of a child's daily life, and if it can conveniently be done just prior to the ritual, it can enhance the entire process.

Location, Location, Location

The most important parts of the pre-bedtime ritual take place in the bedroom. This is where you should set the slower tempo for getting a child ready for sleep. Activities such as tickling, wrestling, seeing how close you can get baby to the ceiling, and other activities that generally work children up – although loving and fun – work against the "wind down" necessary for a good ritual. It is much more effective to adopt a slower tempo as bedtime approaches and to put off the fun-loving stuff until children are under the covers. Then it's merely a matter of creating a loving interaction that continues the wind down, says farewell, and says it with love. For example, you and your child may slowly, ponderously, sleepily say good night to all the stuffed animals, characters that may have been drawn on the wall, and persons who are important to the child. Then you may read some stories, being careful not to read in an arousing, excitable way. This can be tricky. It's important to keep the story interesting but not so interesting that it turns into a potboiler that keeps the child awake long after you want him or her to go to sleep.

Sleepy but Awake

To successfully teach children the skills they need to sleep alone, they must be put in or taken to bed while they are sleepy but still awake. There are two related reasons for this. The first involves sleep stages. A century of sleep science has shown that the sleep of all humans occurs in four stages. The first stage is the lightest and shallowest sleep, and the final stage is the heaviest and deepest sleep. Throughout the night, children cycle through all four stages six to eight times. Each time they rise up to and through stage one, there is a chance they may partially or fully wake up. In order to go back to sleep, they must know how; they must have sleep skills. So children who have been taught that they're okay when they wake up in the middle of the night, and that they don't need to cry or call out for Mom or Dad, will merely go back to sleep. There is little chance they will remember the event in the morning, and because it did not come to the attention of parents, it becomes a "non-event."

Children who do not have such skills wake up and find themselves alone in the dark not knowing what to do. Crying is the inevitable result, and how parents respond starts or contributes to the process that leads to night crying as a behavior problem.

The second reason for putting children to bed sleepy but awake involves "sleep associations." When children are in learning situations – especially ones that can be stressful, like bedtime – they form associations between what is happening and what is present at the time. If children are put in bed asleep, the associations they form when they fall asleep are different from the ones that will be present if they wake up in their bedroom. For example, if you rock your child to sleep in the family room and then place her in bed, she will awake in a completely different situation from where she went to sleep. When your child fell asleep, you and possibly your spouse were present, and the lights and television were on. In the new situation, she is alone in the dark. She will be scared and will probably cry or call out for you. For this reason, the pre-bedtime ritual should end with your sleepy but still awake child in bed with the lights out, which is the exact situation the child will be in if he or she wakes up in the night.

Some parents are tempted to lay down with their child. But this can create an association problem if the child falls asleep knowing that the parent was in the bed. Remember that the goal here is to teach your child to become familiar with and depend on a specific bedtime scenario. A favorite teddy bear, blanket, pillow, and bed arrangement are things that can be part of this scenario. Then if children wake during the night, they can make quick contact with everything that was there when they went to sleep, reassure themselves that all is as it should be, and go back to sleep. If something is missing, going back to sleep will be a little harder, especially if the thing that is missing is important and is obviously gone. If you accidentally or purposely become a part of that group of sleepy-time objects when your child falls asleep, and then leave your child, you will be the most important and obvious thing missing if your child wakes up. When this happens, the child usually will call or cry out so that someone (guess who?) puts everything back the way it was when he or she went to sleep. This is why it is so important for parents to say farewell with love and have the child sleepy but awake when they depart.

Please remember that no matter how well you do this, there is no guarantee that your child will not be upset when you leave the bedroom. But it can ease some of the unpleasant feelings parents usually have when they leave their children for the night. You can rest assured you have done everything possible to help your child successfully make the night voyage he or she is about to embark upon. And your child is more likely to accept the journey with little upset and go to sleep.

Ritual Length

The final item involves how much time to spend in the pre-bedtime ritual. Actually, there is no limit, and you should feel free to spend as much or as little time as you wish. However, there are drawbacks to spending too little time or too much time on a ritual. You should spend enough time to clearly communicate the message I discussed earlier – "Farewell, my love." You also should realize that children quickly become attached to their ritual. That means if you start out spending 45 minutes getting your child ready for bed, he may expect that same amount of time each night. Your goals should be to establish a bedtime ritual that works for you and your child that can be used on a nightly basis.

In many cases, the length of the ritual depends upon how much time is available to you and how long you think it should take to prepare your child for sleep. By the way, time here refers to the time spent after the child is in bed. Many parents think ritual time begins when they first tell their child it is time for bed. The period between this announce-ment and the child getting in bed could include the time it takes for a bath, putting on pajamas, putting toys away, and so on. True, these events are child focused, but I do not count them as part of the pre-bedtime ritual. They simply are tasks the child must complete. The ritual involves parents delivering only love and the only thing the child has to do is receive it. A reasonable in-bed ritual for a young child might last 10 or 15 minutes. The main task is to establish this special time early and stick with it. Once they get used to it, children usually become very attached to their special time with parents before bed, and "short-changing"' them can lead to distress and resistance.

Summary

In conclusion, the pre-bedtime ritual is an opportunity for creativity in the service of love. As indicated, children are going on a long journey alone in the dark and parents merely want to prepare their children for the trip by wishing them well and sending them on their way with love.

Solving Sleep Problems with Infants

Most sleep experts – myself included – recommend no intervention for problems at bedtime for children younger than six months. That does not mean I think children who are six months or older are fair game for mean and cruel treatment at bedtime. Rather, after the age of six months, the overall health, happiness, and developmental progression of children improves to the point where they can sleep for longer periods and handle waking up by themselves.

Remember that children learn through doing things and experiencing some kind of change as a result of what they do. A well-loved and cared for infant has, by the age of six months, learned that crying leads to caring responses from a parent. Crying is something children do well early in

'I'm Crying My Way Back to You'

life. In fact, besides filling their diapers, it is one of the things they do best. Early research by T. Berry Brazleton shows that children at two weeks of age cried as much as two hours a day; that time increased to three hours a day in the weeks that followed. Fortunately, crying time drops to less than an hour a day after the age of two months or so. Unfortunately, for parents trying to get their needed rest, most of this crying takes place at night.

Complicating matters for parents who are teaching their children independent-sleep skills after the age of six months is the fact that their child has had six months to practice exactly the opposite of what parents would like the child to learn. That is, children have had an abundance of experience crying in their cribs and having their parents respond to soothe them. The more loving and caring the parents have been, the more firmly the child has likely learned the connection between crying and being quickly soothed.

Another complication is what I referred to in Chapter 4 as the four stages of sleep. The stages range from the kind of dreamy, hypnotic state that first occurs as a person is descending into full sleep to the deepest stage of sleep where there is no consciousness at all. All of us, children and adults alike, cycle through these stages during the night. And it is highly likely that children will come near to waking up or will actually wake up at least once during the night. This is not a problem when they have learned good sleep onset skills that they can use by themselves. But for some children (especially very young ones), waking up poses a problem they cannot solve on their own. Distressed, they cry out for their parents.

How children summon their parents when they've awakened can pose another problem. True, it is just a cry. But it is not just **any** cry. It is the perfect cry. It has been crafted through hours of practice over the course of the child's young life. Children who are distressed while alone or away from their parents make distressful sounds that I refer to as whimpering and crying. If no one comes and responds to the whimpering and crying, the child adjusts the "quality" of that whimpering and crying so that parents and other important persons are sure to get the message. Depending on how much the child is bothered, the child is usually successful. At that point, the child has learned something very powerful: *This is what it takes. This is the kind of cry that will bring my parents. This is what I need to do if I want them to come.* The child knows he or she has hit upon exactly the right tone, intensity, and quality of crying that parents cannot ignore.

This then will be the kind of crying that is done in the middle of the night. And it can do little good for a sleep expert to tell parents to ignore crying in the middle of the night in order to solve bedtime problems, because the cry they are being asked to ignore has been impossible to ignore time and again. But be that as it may, ignoring crying is a core component to effective treatment of sleep problems in infants.

Here are four strategies that parents can use to address bedtime problems in infants. (I endorse the first two and merely mention the others.)

Ignoring: Cold Turkey

The most effective and, sadly, the most difficult-to-implement strategy is outright ignoring, or the "cold turkey" approach. This approach involves not responding to an infant's crying in a nearby room in the middle of the night. That sentence was very easy to type. The tactic, however, is almost impossible to follow. Nonetheless, I would be remiss if I did not say it is an effective way of solving bedtime problems and does not harm children physically or psychologically. Whether it harms parents physically and psychologically remains to be seen, but I suspect that it does. Bear in mind that doing what I am suggesting goes against everything you have learned about good child care up to this point. Not only am I asking you to violate the connection you and your child have established regarding distress, but I suspect there also may be some violation of evolutionary rules. In other words, a child and a parent have learned and followed a certain pattern of behaviors for when the child is distressed – the child cries, the parent comes. This connection probably has some great survival value. That is, early in the history of our species, it was almost certainly essential for parents to respond to the distress of their infants in order to protect them from a wide range of potentially fatal woes. If this kind of responding to child distress is encoded genetically, and then learned over and over again behaviorally, it is a very hard connection to break.

On the sunny side of this issue is the fact that if a parent convinces his or her spouse this is the way they should go, and they are successful at it, the bedtime problem will almost certainly be solved in three to five nights. But be warned, these will not be ordinary nights. Time spent listening to one's infant cry is time that passes very SLOWLY. And the word "SLOWLY" does not really capture the excruciating tempo I have in mind here. This time passes like molasses poured on a freezing cold day, like the inch-by-inch flow of a frozen river, like the sands of time trickling through a plugged-up hour glass. In other words, it doesn't seem to pass at all!

Einstein, in an attempt to explain the theory of relativity, used the following example: If one is riding on a train for an hour with an interesting person, the hour passes quickly; if one is riding on a train with a dull and boring person, the hour passes very slowly. The kind of slow I am referring to when your child is crying is way, way, way slower than what Einstein was describing on that train with a boring person. When a child begins to cry in the middle of the night, and you decide to stay in bed, it will seem as if time is standing still.

Here's another factor to consider: This slowly passing time and the decision not to respond to the child will almost certainly be harder on one parent than the other. Disagreements and even arguments between parents can result. One parent may say he or she can't take it anymore while the other parent says they must stay strong in order to solve the problem. One parent may even play possum, hoping against hope that his or her act will motivate the other parent to take care of the child. In both kinds of scenarios, both parents lose sleep, and at least one parent inevitably has to get up for work. If these are not grounds for a fight, I don't know what is.

Now the good news: The steps for cold-turkey ignoring are simple and easy to follow. Really, the only step is to completely ignore the crying. How long will it last? While some beleaguered parents have reported trying this option and then listening to their child cry for more than three hours, that situation is unlikely. It is more likely that a very committed child will cry for as long as an hour, then whimper and go to sleep, and then wake up again and cry some more. (I do not challenge parents who report that their child has cried intensely for more than three hours; it is distinctly possible it happened, and even if it didn't it could easily have seemed to them like three hours or even more).

When using ignoring, it can help to check on the child. A cry is a call of distress, and distress is sometimes tied to problems that a parent needs to solve. These include diaper rash, getting caught in the crib, loss of a treasured object, illness, or other situations that are too horrible to even think about. These kinds of concerns can keep parents awake and in distress themselves. For those folks, I recommend a procedure I call the "putter." This is where one parent goes into the child's bedroom and quietly "putters" around in the semi-darkness. If the child's crying slows or lets up even a little, it is unlikely that he or she is experiencing any of the problems that I mentioned. However, a child with diaper rash does not stop crying just because a parent enters the room. The same is true for a child with a fever, stuck feet, lost toys, or a more serious problem. I recommend the putter as a way to assess whether your child actually needs your help. If you can be reassured that your child is okay by puttering, you can continue with the cold-turkey approach.

The main thing to remember about this approach is that it is easy (ignore the crying), it does work (the crying usually stops after three to five nights), and there is a way to check on your child without upsetting the strategy.

Graduated Ignoring: Ferber Method

Graduated ignoring is a method that can be used by folks who have a hard time doing cold-turkey ignoring; in other words, everyone else. The graduated ignoring method was developed by Dr. Richard Ferber and explained in his book, *Solve Your Child's Sleep Problems,* which was mentioned earlier.

In graduated ignoring, parents ignore their crying infant for specific lengths of time that gradually grow longer over the course of the days that they follow their plan. For example, on the first night of the plan, you would ignore the crying for no longer than five minutes. On the second night, the ignoring would last a bit longer, perhaps 10 minutes. Then the ignoring would get longer, perhaps 15 minutes on the third night, 20 minutes on the fourth night, and so forth. I recommend that the top end of the ignoring time be about 45 to 60 minutes.

While this method of slowly increasing the ignoring time is easier than the cold-turkey method, it is not necessarily easy to do. It still involves ignoring the crying child. It still involves not responding to a distress call whose importance has been "encoded" by evolution and months of experience. That still makes it very difficult. Additionally, you must ignore much more crying in graduated ignoring than in cold-turkey ignoring. It may not seem like it to you, but that's because the crying is spread over several days and possibly even a couple of weeks. Some children do indeed cry up to the 45-to-60-minute limit, and then continue to do that for a few days in a row. However, there is an important fact of nature that operates on your side (rather than the infant's side). Specifically, it takes a lot of effort to engage in that kind of crying, and although infants will sometimes cry 45 to 60 minutes for days in a row, it won't be for very many days. There is good research that shows that the graduated ignoring method, within a reasonable amount of time of one to two weeks, eliminates or dramatically reduces bedtime problems in these very young children.

When using graduated ignoring, you can visit your child's room to comfort and quiet him or her. There are some steps to follow, or at least keep in mind, during these visits that enhance the overall effectiveness of the plan. Specifically, when you visit the room at the end of the time that has been established for that night, you should interact as little as possible when soothing the infant. It is actually best if you do not speak or pick up the child. Yes, the object of the visit is to provide reassurance and soothing, but it should only be a minimal amount, just enough to calm your child and reassure you. Remember that the primary objective is to help children eventually learn to manage on their own the distress that occurs upon waking and to get themselves back to sleep without our help.

Sharing the Family Bed

Sharing the family bed is a procedure that involves allowing the infant to sleep in bed with the parents. There are clear advantages to this method, including the almost complete absence of distress for the child if he or she wakes up during the night. Also, there is typically little distress as the child is put to bed at night. It is almost as if children have been allowed to enter the gates of paradise for the evening, and that act alone calms them, soothes them, and pleases them beyond measure. Although this may seem golden, please consider the possibility that it may be fool's gold.

There are a variety of reasons why parents may not want to have a third (or fourth, fifth, or sixth) party in their bed at night. Here are a few of the biggest ones:

- **Parents rolling over.** This can be tragic. In 1999, The Centers for Disease Control reported in the *Archives of Pediatrics and Adolescent Medicine* (Sept. 29) that between January 1990 and December 1997, 515 children under the age of 2 years died as a result of co-sleeping with adults in an adult bed. The fatalities occurred either because the adult accidentally either rolled over on a child or bumped a child out of bed. True, this is more likely to happen when a parent is intoxicated or in some other way impaired, but it can happen with a deeply sleeping adult who is merely trying to get a good night's rest. This is a rare event. But it is nonetheless real and a risk that goes along with using the family bed as a way to solve infant sleep problems.

- **Disrupted schedules.** The child's sleep schedule may not match the parents' sleep schedule. And if everyone is in the same bed, the person with the most disruptive schedule is likely to control the schedule of the others. This may cause distress, limit rest, and be more of a hassle than parents are willing to bear once they discover what a hassle it is. Please note too that children quickly become attached to this procedure, so breaking the habit can be difficult. Parents who decide to use the family bed plan, and then discover a week or two later that it won't work, now have a bigger problem than the one they had before they chose to use the family bed.

- **Complete lack of privacy.** Without going into great detail, there are times when married adults prefer to have private moments in their own bed at night. However, if parents have chosen to share the family bed to train sleep skills to their infant, the possibility of privacy becomes pretty small. There are ways to get around this issue, but it still needs to be considered as a possible problem.

Overall, sharing the family bed does have some advantages. But its disadvantages probably outweigh them. Sleep research indicates that physicians are unlikely to prescribe this as way to solve infant bedtime problems. (Physicians tend to recommend a variation on ignoring.) Nonetheless, for those parents who are willing to commit themselves to the necessary schedule restrictions and cautions that must be imposed for this plan, sharing the family bed may be a viable option.

Medication

This option involves using medication that induces sleepiness in the infant. I do not endorse this particular option, but physicians occasionally prescribe it, and parents sometimes turn to it. This is, at best, an option of last resort, and should be used, if at all, for only very limited periods of time.

There are at least three problems with using medication for solving sleep problems with children and, particularly, with infants. First, there are virtually no medications that induce sleepiness without other risky side effects. Also, it is easy to give a child too much of these medications.

Second, the use of medication to solve bedtime problems typically involves some kind of "rebound." A rebound refers to an increase in symptoms that surpass those of the pretreatment level after treatment has ended. For example, various nasal sprays reduce nasal congestion and provide immediate relief, but are accompanied by congestion that is worse than the congestion that led to the use of the spray in the first place. Similarly, using medication to solve bedtime problems can increase sleeplessness and distress beyond pre-medication levels if the medication is used for more than a few days.

The third problem with using medication involves learning. I emphasized in an earlier chapter that children learn through doing something, then experiencing a change. This process results in patterns of behavior that are strengthened over time. The pattern I hope parents can establish in their children is for them to be able to resolve sleep problems on their own and develop a healthy, independent sleep habit. This process requires children to induce their own sleepiness. Using medication eliminates the possibility that infants can practice inducing their own sleepiness because it is induced for them. In effect, an infant who comes to rely on medications to get sleepy is denied the opportunity to learn this valuable skill. When the medication is no longer used, the infant is right back where he or she started.

Summary

Listening to your infant cry in bed is one of the hardest things you will do. Resisting the urge to jump up and run into the nursery every time your baby cries takes tremendous strength and willpower. But ignoring and graduated ignoring are effective ways to teach infants basic sleep skills. While there are some other alternative methods to use with infants, the ignoring approaches are probably the safest and most reliable. It will be tough, but hang in there!

CHAPTER 6

Solving Sleep Problems with Toddlers

When it comes to sleep problems with toddlers, they have the same capacity as infants to thwart parental intentions, undermine parental confidence, and recruit parental indulgence, plus a few more tactics that infants can't use. In other words, solving sleep problems with toddlers can be even more difficult than solving sleep problems with infants.

'I'm Crying and Crawling My Way Back to You'

Toddlers pose a triple threat. They can cry, call out, and come out. Their crying usually triggers parental sympathies, guilt, learning-based problem solutions, and genetically determined survival responses – the same parental emotions and responses infant crying triggers. They can call out using words to make their demands known.

And they can actually get out of bed, open the bedroom door, and crawl or toddle out to skirt and protest bedtime rules.

In this chapter, I'll discuss each of these areas and how to address them.

Crying

Like infants, toddlers will cry after a "Good night" and lights out because they want the lights on and to be with their parents. However, a toddler's wails may not pack the punch they used to when the child was an infant because Mom and Dad are more accustomed to it and can handle it better. A toddler still can bring Mom and Dad running, mind you, but crying is substantially less powerful.

When your toddler cries at or after bedtime, you can use some of the same strategies that work so well with infants.

Ignoring: Cold Turkey Approach

Clearly, the most powerful way to solve toddlers' bedtime crying is to ignore it completely. This tends to be easier with toddlers than with crying infants. But it still can be difficult. Due to the always-active learning processes in children, it is best for you to decide the method you are going to use and commit to it before you try it. Otherwise, you could be using a strategy that is not effective or actually does the opposite of what you want. When ignoring doesn't work, it's usually because parents use it only sporadically, sometimes responding to a child's crying and sometimes ignoring it. When this happens, kids soon learn how to "beat the system" by crying even more until a parent comes. Then parents can become frustrated and give up. So while ignoring is a good option when used correctly, it still carries some risks.

Graduated Ignoring: Ferber Method

I discussed how to use the Ferber Method with infants in Chapter 5. It can be used in essentially the same way with toddlers.

Positive Routines

Positive routines is a procedure based on the principle of momentum. (This is from physics, so it really is scientific.) The principle states that the momentum of a moving object determines how much resistance is necessary to stop its forward progress. As it turns out, a variety of scientific studies show the same is true for child behavior. When child behavior, such as following parental commands, has a forward momentum (the child regularly obeys the commands), new commands are less likely to generate resistance than commands that are issued when no momentum is present. In other words, if a child is likely to follow instructions to do a number of things because they are fun or easy or both, a sort of momentum builds up. Once that momentum is established, the likelihood that the child will follow a command that is not as fun or easy goes way up because that command is "captured" by the momentum that was started through the easy or fun commands. With positive routines, the strategy is merely to give a number of commands for activities that children are highly likely to do immediately, and then blend in commands that might not be so popular.

Routines always work best if they are directed toward bedtime, bringing the child closer and closer to meeting the requirements actually necessary for getting into bed. The logic here is to use easy and fun commands that involve bedtime events, such as getting a book or a teddy bear or a drink or hugs, and then getting into bed. The point is to get children moving in response to parental commands and then to drop in the command to "go to bed" as the child's momentum – their compliance rate – goes up.

For example, this might be a typical series of tasks:

- Let's stand up.
- Let's walk to the kitchen.
- Let's walk to the bedroom stairs.
- Give me a hug.
- Let's walk to the top of the stairs.
- Give me another hug.
- Let's walk into your bedroom.
- Let's put jammies on your teddy bear.
- Let's put jammies on you.
- Let's pick out a book.
- Let's sit on the bed.
- Let's get under the covers.
- Let's read a story together.
- Give me a hug.
- Let's say good night.

Again, the idea here is to build a momentum and then drop in a major instruction to go to bed at the end. While it may seem as though your child could figure out what you're doing, the evidence indicates that toddlers don't see through it very well. In order for it to work, you must make the routine upbeat, positive, and fun. With each task the child completes, you should be enthusiastic, appreciative, and loving. These kinds of parental responses trigger the mechanisms of learning that I discussed in Chapter 3, and also can lead to a kind of behavioral "take off" that makes it more likely that the child will go to bed and stay there.

Parents who use positive routines to solve bedtime problems with toddlers should select and use whatever tasks their child can easily do and instructions they know their child is likely to follow prior to bedtime. Then, it's merely a matter of chaining the tasks together and leading up to the ultimate instruction to go to bed.

Sharing the Family Bed

Sharing the family bed is another treatment option for bedtime problems with toddlers. Just as with infants, this strategy has disadvantages and advantages. While it is less likely that a parent will roll over on a toddler and cause injury because toddlers are bigger, it can still happen. There's also the loss of privacy for the parents, and the problems with different sleep and waking schedules for Mom, Dad, and the child. On the plus side, allowing a toddler to sleep in your bed can reduce or end crying at bedtime and lead to a good night's sleep for everyone.

While I do not often recommend sharing the family bed as a treatment option, I do recognize that some families may prefer it. For those families, if they are willing to follow through and adjust schedules so that the family bed option can work, bedtime crying can be resolved.

Medication

It is worth noting that medication is also a treatment option for toddlers with bedtime problems. But for the same reasons I cited with infants, it is not one I endorse or recommend.

Calling Out

A behavior toddlers can do that infants can't is calling out from the bedroom. These calls can be a combination of requests, complaints, and sometimes threats. Requests can be for visits from a parent or a drink, answers to questions, or solutions to problems. The complaints can involve illness ("My stomach hurts"), fears ("I heard a noise in the closet"), discomfort ("I'm hot" or "I'm cold"), bed concerns ("My blanket fell on the floor"), and a variety of other issues, manufactured and real, that a toddler can conjure up when facing the seemingly dreadful prospect of going to bed on his or her own. Problem solution requests can cover a broad range of issues ("What time is it?"; What time do I have to get up?"; "What am I going to wear tomorrow?").

This situation requires the same type of approaches that are used when children cry (cold-turkey ignoring, graduated ignoring, positive routines, and, to a much lesser extent, sharing the family bed).

Coming Out

As if crying out and calling out weren't enough of a problem for beleaguered parents, toddlers have another weapon in their arsenal of mass disruption. They can also come out of their room after they have been put in bed for the night. This can be particularly troubling because children who do this usually are very successful at deterring their parents when they try to solve the problem. The results can be heated discussions, physical interactions, altercations, and even some gamesmanship on the child's part. Different options are needed for these situations.

Early Warning System

Some children are sneaky about coming out of their room, so it is important for parents to know when they are making their break. If the bedroom is out of your sight, then it is important for you to come up with a way to know when your child crosses the room threshold. One easy way to do this is to attach a shop owner's bell to the doorframe so that the bell rings when the door is opened. If you are more electronically sophisticated, you might even use an electronic eye system that sets off a beeper, an alarm, or a tornado alert. (Parents who are willing to go to the extreme of hooking up a tornado alert will probably find that it only has to be used once or twice to have the desired effect.) If you choose not to use some sort of mechanical early warning system, you will have to keep a close eye out for your "fugitives" from the bedroom and capture them as quickly as possible for a return to bed.

The early warning system works even if you decide to leave your toddler's bedroom door slightly open.

Robotic Return

How a parent who has captured a bedroom escapee acts is an important part of solving the "coming out" problem. Remember the rules for learning that I discussed in Chapter 3? Typically, children engage in behaviors that are followed by positive events they like; they tend to avoid or not use behaviors that are followed by negative events they don't like. They learn through experience, with pleasant experiences leading to increases in a behavior and unpleasant experiences leading to decreases. If a toddler escapes from the bedroom and encounters a pleasant, talkative, affectionate, or otherwise pleasing parent, the child is likely to make a connection that you don't want them to make. Specifically, he or she may learn that leaving the bedroom and encountering a parent is a lot more fun than being in the room alone. That's why I recommend what I call a "robotic return."

In this strategy, the fugitive encounters a parent who looks like Mommy or Daddy, but walks more stiffly, treats the situation seriously and solemnly, and has no voice box. While returning the child to the bedroom, the parent says nothing. (By nothing, I mean total and absolute silence.) Many parents will be tempted to bark, yell, or scream at their child, or issue commands; I strongly urge them not to do it. Remember that children don't like to experience nothing; in fact, they often prefer being yelled at, criticized, or talked to sternly because it is better than the "nothing" of being ignored or being in bed alone. To avoid giving the child the attention he or she wants, I recommend that you behave like a robot that doesn't talk and merely return your child to his or her bedroom. The less stimulation you provide, the better the result.

I also recommend that you close the bedroom door again after you've returned your child to bed. Your child will probably cry because he or she wants that door to be open. But closing the door is a learning-based consequence that reduces the chances that the child will try to escape again. Eventually your child will begin to understand that leaving the bedroom will result in the door being closed once he or she is returned to bed. I recommend that you open the child's bedroom door as soon as the crying (or pleading, demanding, begging, etc.) stops. If the child tries to leave the bedroom again, you should use the robotic return, then close the door and leave it shut until morning.

Holding the Door

Once your child is back in bed, and the bedroom door is closed, he or she may attempt to open it. In such cases, it may be necessary for you to hold the door shut. This can be exasperating and tiring for parents, and it may take a while before your child stops trying to open the door. Nonetheless, it is important to stand fast and, for lack of a better word, **WIN**. If your child wins, he or she has learned how to defeat you at your own game and probably will be emboldened in his or her campaign against bedtime.

I do not recommend locking children's bedroom doors to keep them inside. It is possible that something could happen in the home (fire, tornado) that would require everyone to get out or to go to a certain part of the house. If a room is locked and the other family members can't get to it to let the person out, results could be tragic. While it is important for parents to solve their child's bedtime problems, the safety of all family members must come first.

By All Means, Do Not Do This

I want to re-emphasize the point I made earlier about remaining silent when returning a child to the bedroom. By all means, do not get into a debate, argument, discussion, reasoning session with, or make threats or promises to, a child who has left his or her bedroom at night. Even if it sounds like children are listening to reason, they are merely playing for time and are actually learning that leaving their bedroom after bedtime is an activity that leads to preferred events. I cannot stress enough how important it is to be absolutely silent while returning a toddler to the bedroom.

Summary

Toddlers pose a new and greater challenge to parents when it comes to going to and staying in bed. With age comes the ability to vocalize and mobilize bedtime protests, which requires parents to revise their approach to the problem. With toddlers, being firm and consistent, and "sticking to your guns" is essential when they cry out, call out, and break out. Remember that the less stimulation you provide in the way of talking, scolding, or otherwise responding to your toddler's pleas, the more quickly he or she will learn the sleep behaviors you are trying to teach.

CHAPTER 7

Solving Sleep Problems with Preschoolers

Preschoolers with sleep problems have at their disposal all the tactics toddlers use to thwart their parents' attempts to establish a good bedtime, and then some.

'I Don't Want to Go to Bed, and You Can't Make Me'

And while the plaintive cry of a preschooler who is unhappy about being in bed doesn't tug as hard at a parent's heartstrings as one from an infant or toddler, preschoolers have their own ways of resisting – usually on the front end of the bedtime process. In other words, preschoolers put up a tougher fight when it comes to actually going to bed.

In this chapter, I'll look at some ways to train preschoolers to comply with bedtime and minimize their resistance. I'll address each of the primary problems preschoolers present at bedtime and once they are in bed, and prescribe some effective ways to address them.

Stalling, Resisting, Avoiding, Running Away

These are the primary areas where a preschooler's skills and sometimes mischievous intentions are vastly superior to those of younger children. Most preschoolers already have a long history of deciding what they want to do and what they don't want to do, and how to follow through. So the most successful of their tactics are subtle ones – preschoolers stall, avoid, or make it seem as if they are really on their way to bed when in fact they are doing as much as they can to avoid going anywhere near it. These subtle tactics often operate a bit below parental radar, and can successfully render a set bedtime meaningless. Other tactics are more blatant and are easier for parents to pick up on, but often still immobilize parental resources because they are a direct challenge to parental authority. Regardless of the tactic, parents can deal with them in a common manner. I will identify three ways.

Direct Commands

This is a time-honored, often-used, and seldom successful tactic. The biggest reason direct commands don't work is because they are not as direct as parents would like to think. Variations on "Would you?" "Could you?" and "Could I coax you to...?" are not in any way, shape, or form, direct. To make direct commands at bedtime truly direct, you must adopt these behaviors: Make and keep eye contact with your child and, in as few words as possible, give a command that is the same as, or at least means the same as, "Go to bed now." The command doesn't have to be said angrily or threateningly, only firmly. Obviously, it is a good idea to forewarn your child that the command is about to occur. You can signal the command by reminding children that it is time to collect their toys, put away their papers, set aside their books, and generally prepare their play or work stations for another day. For example, you can say, "Tommy, it's time to start getting ready for bed. Please pick up your toys and books now."

Unfortunately, if bedtime problems have lasted through the toddler years into preschool and beyond, other forms of resistance or noncompliance are likely to occur. As a result, the child may choose not to obey the parent's command to get ready for bed. This moves us to another area and another approach to the problem.

When Children Resist Commands

When faced with a command to prepare for bed, the shrewd bedtime avoider will often play deaf, move to another room, or find other ways to ignore or blow off the parental command. In a sense, the child is gambling; flaunting parental authority carries with it a high risk for a disciplinary response. But there is no real gamble here because, as I've said before, the child who truly wants to avoid bedtime would rather have "something" – the parent's attention, even if it is in the form of punishment or other negative responses – than the "nothing" of being in bed alone. The child, who resists parental commands to prepare for bed, and who is disciplined with something like a time-out, is actually receiving a consequence that he or she prefers over going to bed.

The first step toward solving this potential problem is merely to recognize it. That is, just because a child has been placed in time-out does

not mean that it is an unpleasant experience for
him or her. As you will recall, learning occurs as
a result of the consequence that follows a child's
behavior. The direction children's learning takes
is governed by how they view the consequence.
If the consequence is something they don't like
or would prefer not to have happen, they are less
likely to repeat the behavior that led to that consequence. However, if the behavior results in a consequence they like or prefer, they are more likely
to use the behavior again. In the bedtime scenario,
the child who earns a time-out for not complying
with a parental command to get ready for bed is
in a situation he or she actually prefers over the
imminent alternative – bedtime. In other words, a
time-out is better than time in bed. Therefore, the
child is in a sense being rewarded. And this reward
makes it more likely that the child will resist bedtime – despite the cost – in the future.

Addressing this problem is pretty easy: Just
use the bed as a "penalty box." For example, if
your child refuses to clean up his toys when you
tell him to get ready for bed, leave the toys where
they are, allow for a minimum amount of pre-
bedtime preparation (brushing teeth, putting on

pajamas), physically guide your child to bed (lead him by the hand to bed, and if necessary, lift him into bed), say good night, and close the door. The following day, at a time that is more important to your child than you (for example, right before his favorite cartoons are about to come on), you can instruct him to put away the things that were left out from the previous night. The consequence of having to do a chore at a time when your child would rather being doing something fun will eventually reduce the behavior of trying to delay or avoid going to bed.

More About Direct Commands

As I've said, I recommend that you begin the direct-command process by telling your child that it's time to get ready for bed. This gives the child an opportunity to get his or her things in order. I also recommend that any resistance to that preparation command be dealt with in the way I have suggested.

If children actually do follow the "get-ready" command, and put their things away, but then resist the actual command to go to bed, I recommend a similar procedure. That is, you dramatically shorten the usual bedtime ritual and put the child directly in bed.

When children actually follow the commands – they go through their bedtime preparation and then put themselves in bed – I recommend that you reward them with a richly affectionate bedtime procedure: lots of hugs and kisses, high-fives, and a real celebration of the child's accomplishment. I have already emphasized the importance of the bedtime ritual in a previous chapter, but in my view, it really can't be emphasized too much.

Consequences and Physical Guidance

In this small section, I want to stress the point that you can use appropriate and gentle-but-firm physical guidance to put your child in bed. This becomes necessary when you have given your child the direct command to get ready for bed, and have had to repeat it once because he or she did not comply. Also, I recommend that you use a consequence that involves eliminating or shortening the bedtime procedure. If there is no consequence, your child is likely to resist instructions to get ready for bed or go to bed night after night because there is no apparent penalty for doing otherwise.

Please note that weaving its way through this entire book is an emphasis on how children learn, and various suggestions for how you can take advantage of this process to teach lessons about bedtime that you desperately want your child to master. In this instance, children who resist bedtime and must be physically guided to their bedrooms and placed in bed, should have a penalty that decreases their resistance. Rather than scolding or withdrawing privileges, I recommend that you take away or cut back on something your child really looks forward to or likes. The bedtime ritual is the logical choice because it is something children universally enjoy.

Crying, Calling Out, and Coming Out

Sadly for parents, in addition to stalling, resisting, avoiding, and running away, preschoolers will also cry, call out, or come out of their rooms after parents say good night for the same reason toddlers cry, call out, and come out of their rooms after bedtime. Specifically, they want to be up and with their parents or, barring that, just up, or, barring that, just have the lights (or television) on. (For that matter, having a pizza delivered would also go a long way toward quieting a preschooler's nocturnal complaints.)

Although preschoolers can be more strenuous in their crying, it is typically less heart-rending and therefore easier for parents to ignore. (Do you notice that the older kids get, the easier it is to ignore nighttime crying?) However, preschoolers who cry excessively at night can easily aggravate their parents, resulting in an angry exchange between parent and child. Multiply the aggravation caused by crying with the irritation triggered by calling out, especially when the calling out is accompanied by some devilishly strategic vocal "button pushing" (for example, "I hate you," "You're not my mother; my real mother wouldn't do this to me"), and the fuse is prepared for some real parental anger. Add in a few instances of coming out of the bedroom, and the fuse has been lit. With a few exceptions, it is my experience that angry exchanges with upset preschoolers rarely make bedtime situations better in either the long run or the short run. As with younger children, it is best for parents to ride out their preschoolers' crying jags and their calling-out campaigns with little or no intervention.

The other methods for managing crying, calling out, and coming out of the bedroom for toddlers also work well with preschoolers who exhibit the same problem. The age difference between toddlers and preschoolers is not large enough to warrant major differences in procedures, so ignoring, graduated ignoring, positive routines, family bed, and medication can be used in about the same way with both. Additionally, the early warning system, robotic return, holding the door, and caveats about maintaining absolute silence with a child who comes out of the bedroom after bedtime also apply for preschoolers. (See Chapter 6 for a review of those recommendations.)

However, as if God or Mother Nature, or both, recognized that there is only so much parents can take from bedtime-resistant children, there are three additional techniques that can work with these older children, and they are clever and fun to use. The first involves positive routines, a technique discussed at length in the chapter on toddlers. Due to increases in preschoolers' language skills, positive routines may work even better with them than toddlers. The other two are the "bedtime pass" and "The Sleep Fairy."

The Bedtime Pass

The bedtime pass has been scientifically tested with children between the ages of 3 and 10, and has routinely been shown to successfully encourage children who historically have resisted going to bed to follow bedtime rules.

The pass is a laminated piece of paper with the words "Bedtime Pass" on it. Lamination is not necessary, but it protects the pass so it lasts longer. (The pass also can be any object your child can hold in his or her hands. In one case, parents used a string of beads that could be hung on the child's bedroom door.)

The procedure involves a simple bargain between you and your child. You give your child a bedtime pass once he or she is in bed, and encourage him or her to keep it somewhere safe. You then tell your child that he or she will be allowed to exchange the pass for one easily satisfied request after the lights are out and you have left the bedroom. Easily satisfied requests include getting a drink of water, getting a hug, having a parent do one quick check of the bedroom, or getting a look at the clothes you have laid out for the child for the next day. Easily satisfied requests do not include playing Monopoly until all the hotels are sold, watching TV until the 1-900 commercials come on, or completing a thousand-piece jigsaw puzzle. In short, the request must be something specific that can be satisfied with a simple action. Once you have carried out the request, the child must surrender the pass. If the child does not use the pass for a request on a particular evening, he or she hangs on to it for the next night.

In my experience, both clinically and scientifically, bedtime passes regularly produce very positive results. Initially, children routinely use the pass. Younger preschoolers – ages 3 to 4 – sometimes need to be trained to give up the pass without a struggle once they've used it, but after a couple of exchanges, the system typically runs pretty smoothly.

An interesting outcome of the procedure is that some children don't use the pass at all. Why this happens is still a mystery. One possibility is that they are saving it up for a rainy day, so to speak. For example, they may be thinking, "I sure would hate not to have my pass if the boogie man comes to my bedroom." Another possibility is that the pass provides children with the comfort of knowing they can use it whenever they want. This feeling, coupled with the typically present fatigue, results in children drifting off to sleep before they can make an exchange. Whatever the reason, when children do not use the pass and drift off to sleep, it's a success for both parent and child.

The Sleep Fairy

The sleep fairy is a clever variation of the traditional tooth fairy story, used to assuage the concerns of children losing baby teeth for generations. The Sleep Fairy is the main character in a book by the same name, written by Janie Peterson; the book's use has been evaluated in a scientific study by Dr. Brett Kuhn, Raymond Burke, and Janie Peterson. It involves putting children in bed and then reading the sleep fairy story from Peterson's book (or inventing a similar story and reciting it to them). The story is simple and sweet: The Sleep Fairy visits children in bed, tells them they are safe, secure, and loved, and promises that if they stay in bed and go to sleep, she will leave a small treat under their pillow. If the children have a good night and go to sleep, parents place a small treat (sticker, small toy, candy) under the pillow for the children to find when they wake up.

Summary

Preschoolers present their own unique problems when it comes to going to bed and going to sleep. While some of the bedtime skills and methods that work well with toddlers can still be used with preschoolers, other more advanced approaches may be necessary for kids in this age group. These include direct commands, positive routines, bedtime passes, and the sleep fairy story. As children get older, they often become more sophisticated in their resistance to bedtime. But they also are better able to understand and positively respond to the more advanced bedtime strategies you use.

CHAPTER 8

Solving Bedtime Problems with Elementary School-Aged Children

For elementary school-aged children who present problems at bedtime, there's both good news and bad news. On the positive side, most children this age typically have abandoned prolonged displays of sadness that include a lot of crying, and are less likely to try to make their parents feel guilty about putting them to bed. On the negative side, these kids are smarter and more sophisticated when it comes to thwarting parents, prolonging bedtimes, frustrating efforts to put them to bed, and inducing temporary or semi-permanent parental surrender. For parents,

'I'll Go to Bed in a Minute – a Really, Really Long Minute'

this can mean that frustration and anger replace the feelings of guilt they felt when dealing with a crying infant who wouldn't go to sleep.

Children in elementary school will resist bedtime with new tactics, including negotiation, overscheduling, delaying, and outright defiance. In this chapter, I'll look at each of these and discuss ways you can respond in order to set and enforce bedtimes and still preserve a loving relationship with your child.

Negotiation

The most socially adapted and effective way elementary school-aged children resist bedtime may appear to parents, on the surface, to be a rational, plausible explanation for why their child shouldn't have go to bed when instructed. Depending on their relationship with their parents, children will explain either patiently or impatiently that they fully intend to go to bed momentarily, but they just have a few tasks to take care of first. As they make their case, they inevitably try to negotiate a small relaxation (or a large one, if they think they can get away with it) of the previously established bedtime. Although the tasks the youngster must complete may seem routine to parents, effective child negotiators have no trouble making them rise to the level of national importance. Unaware parents may actually exceed the child's wishes by blaming themselves for not recognizing how serious these tasks are. But a closer look at the situation will reveal that the child is being manipulative, the "negotiation" is a sham, and the child is dramatically exaggerating the importance of the tasks. The child does not want to go to bed, and if he or she can string Dad and Mom along by pretending to be busy with important activities, and end up going to bed later, that's what he or she will try to do.

The best way to counter negotiation is to leave the bargaining table. That is, avoid getting involved in the negotiation at all. If a bedtime has been set, it is reasonable and prudent for you to enforce it, so the time your child actually spends in bed is approximately the time you chose for him or her to be there.

True, emergencies can occur, but they are rare; the resistant child creates a sense of emergency on a regular basis. He or she may say that homework or school projects must be completed before bedtime, books must be finished, television programs must be viewed until they're over, e-mail messages must be sent, and clothing for the following day must be laid out. All of these tasks are legitimate child concerns, but they are rarely legitimate bedtime emergency concerns. If you give in to your child by extending bedtime, you provide no incentive for him or her to solve related problems during waking hours. Leaving any or all problems or chores unresolved for one night gives kids an incentive to resolve them on a timelier basis the next day. When this happens, children are likely to be upset and feel that the parent is being unfair. My recommendation to you is to get used to it; it is likely to get worse before it gets better. Unfortunately, part of being a parent involves enforcing rules, the merit of which will not be clear to children until they become parents. Be that as it may, it is important in the area of bedtime that you stand your ground. There are two primary reasons for this. First, children must get adequate rest. If they are left on their own to decide this, it probably won't happen. Second, children are always learning. Whatever they do regularly, they learn to do better. So if they are regularly learning to successfully resist bedtime, they generally will get better at resisting. A successful bedtime resister becomes good not only at resisting bedtime, but also at resisting parents in other areas.

I am not recommending that you blow a whistle like a basketball referee and abruptly end negotiations. When a child asks for just a few minutes more, it's okay to say "Okay" as long as it is just a few minutes. But this should occur only once in an evening, and the child should be either sent or taken to bed when you decide time is up.

Overscheduling

A major problem in modern child-rearing involves overscheduling. Children have soccer games, birthday parties, club meetings, outings, school activities, and their many friends. As a result, some perfectly reasonable deadlines, such as a regular bedtime, are not met. (Children get home late, dinner is eaten late, homework doesn't get done, and so on.) It's difficult enough when there is only one child in the family, but it gets even tougher when parents are trying to keep track of more kids. Although the best advice is for parents to schedule children's activities so that these kinds of things don't happen regularly, I fully recognize that this is easier said than done, especially when there is more than one child in the family. Be that as it may, my best advice for limiting bedtime problems caused by overscheduling is to simply reduce the number of activities.

Sometimes, emergencies will arise when, for any variety of reasons, your child hasn't done his or her homework or a school project, hasn't finished daily chores, or hasn't taken care of other responsibilities. When your child uses these situations as excuses or reasons for not going to bed on time, you must determine whether it is a true emergency that requires some flexibility in bedtime rules or just a way for the child to put off or get out of going to bed. The key here is that you – not your child – make the decision. Some adjustment in your child's schedule also might be necessary to prevent such conflicts from happening in the future.

Delaying

Delaying is a tactic children sometimes use as part of negotiation. This is more of a passive than an active strategy, and it's sometimes hard to spot. A typical scenario involves a parent reminding a child that it's time for bed, and the child making virtually no movement to follow the bedtime request. Instead, the child becomes more involved in whatever he or she was doing than when the request was made. If the child detects urgency in the parent's request, he or she might appear to be putting away toys or getting ready for bed. But often this is just a cover, and the child will do it only while the parent can still see him or her. As soon as the parent, satisfied that he or she has fulfilled the parental duty of reminding you-know-who that it's bedtime, is out of sight or not watching, the child resumes his or her original activity, pleased that a momentary distraction has been dealt with successfully. These child tactics and parental responses can actually lead to a drawn-out series of chess-like "moves" between the parent and child that eventually results in the parent getting angry. This is an unfortunate event, because to be truly successful, a good bedtime should involve an expression of love between a parent and child who won't see each other again until daybreak or later. If one of them becomes extremely angry, this contaminates that expression of love. Therefore, it is best to nip this tactic in the bud.

Delaying tactics work because parents don't sufficiently assert their authority on the front end of these kinds of exchanges. Just saying the words that are part of a command is not the same thing as commanding a child. Although this book is not about instructional control, instructional control is a very important part of the message. In order for instructional control to actually be established during training so that the child will obey future instructions, you must make the instructions clear and specific so that the child can understand them. If you merely remind your child that it's just about bedtime when you actually want him or her to get ready for bed, your child may not truly understand what you want. In these situations, children may believe, on some level of their consciousness, that the parent only wants them to know that bedtime is close and not that they should actually do anything about it. Thus, they may feel perfectly justified in continuing their activity as if nothing has happened. My main message here for you, as a parent, is to be clear and to enforce any commands you make. For example, if your child is playing with her toys when you tell her to get ready for bed, it's best to make eye contact with her, very clearly announce that bedtime is in five minutes, and clearly state that anything that's not picked up within that time will have to be left out until morning or will be taken away for a period of time as a consequence. You could use other approaches, but this one is consistent with my main message and, usually, is most effective. The bottom line is that delaying only happens if you allow it. I recommend that you do not.

Defiance

A much more serious bedtime problem with elementary school children involves outright defiance. In this scenario, you may have been very clear in your command, yet your child makes no move at all to comply. In other words, your child decides to stand his or her ground, come what may. The child is unafraid of or undeterred by your parental authority. True, there is some element of defiance in bedtime resistance at younger ages, but when it occurs in elementary school children, it's a different sort of child behavior. Defiance can lead parents to resort to punishment or other physical intervention (e.g., spanking the child or dragging the child to bed by the arm). When this regularly happens, parents may be dealing with a bigger problem than bedtime resistance.

Training, Training, Training

Did I mention training? Children who actively resist bedtime through confrontation with a parent ultimately will need some kind of training in behavioral management. The target of this training is instructional control, and achieving it involves building on the concepts of learning that I described earlier in the book. Since the focus of this book is children's sleep and bedtime problems, I won't go into a detailed description of this process. However, at the end of the book you will find a number of books and other resources that can provide information about instructional control training for resistant children.

Other Reasons for Resistance

It is possible that a child who is resisting going to bed is merely tired and grouchy. In technical terms, fatigue deteriorates neural controls, which are necessary to process and follow commands. So as children become more and more tired, they are less and less able to follow parental instructions. If children are misbehaving regularly at bedtime, it is likely they are either going to bed too late or getting up too early. In other words, a little more rest may be all that's needed to solve the problem.

Another possible reason for resistance is a history of parental wavering when it comes to commands. It is possible that parents have adopted a "Would you? Could you? Could I coax you to?" type of strategy to get kids in bed, and that the kids have actively and successfully resisted that method. As I said earlier, as children continue to engage in certain behaviors, they get better at those behaviors. So if their behavior regularly involves resistance, they get better at resisting. If that scenario is the basis for a child's current resistance, then all that may be needed is a much firmer parental stand along with some kind of enforcement procedures.

Typically, when I talk about enforcement procedures, I mean costs and benefits. The "costs" are the negative consequences – loss of privileges (TV, snacks, play time), losing a favorite toy for a certain period of time, time-out, etc. – for not meeting parental expectations. The "benefits" are the positive consequences – a treat, extra time playing video games, doing something special with Mom or Dad – for meeting parental expectations. For bedtime problems, costs and benefits could be in the form of red tickets and green tickets that have a specific amount of time written on them (e.g., 10 minutes, 15 minutes, 20 minutes, etc.). Red tickets are given to the child when he or she resists going to bed, and green tickets are given when the child goes to bed on time without resistance. So if your child resists and you give him a red ticket with "15 minutes" on it, he must go to bed 15 minutes earlier than the regular bedtime the next night. If your child follows instructions to go to bed, and you give him a green ticket with "20 minutes" written on it, he gets to go to bed 20 minutes later on a weekend night. The main point here is that you are supplying direct feedback as an incentive to motivate your child to stop resisting bedtime and start following bedtime instructions. (If resistance is being caused by more serious reasons than I have discussed, professional help may be necessary to expedite or expand instructional control.)

Playing Within the Bedroom

A problem that tends to emerge with elementary school-aged children is playing or reading in the bedroom after they've gone to bed. My opinion about this is that as long as the lights are out, toys are put away, all electronic devices except the alarm clock are turned off or unplugged, and the noise from the playing can't be heard outside the bedroom door, such playing should be permitted.

At a recent workshop I attended, participants were told that they could sleep during the presentations as long as they sat upright in their chairs with their feet in front of them and their head directly above their shoulders. The humor of this announcement quickly became clear as participants who tried to sleep in this position found it impossible. Similarly, with the rules I have in mind, a child trying to play or read in a dark bedroom is so close to impossible that the problem should quickly be resolved. Enforcing these rules may not be as difficult as you think. It may merely involve ensuring the lights are off in the bedroom (a night light is okay), putting favorite toys out of reach, removing radios or televisions, and not letting your child have a flashlight or other sources of bright light. Keep in mind that a bedtime is selected because children are tired at about that time. If they are in a dimly lit or dark room with nothing to do, they will fall asleep. Whatever they play with in their room is what keeps them awake; take those things away, and sleep is likely to follow.

Summary

Bedtime for elementary school-aged children can become a battle of wills and endurance – if you let it. By the time your child reaches this age, you know him or her pretty well, and he or she knows what to expect from you. That's why firmness and calmness in the face of such tactics as negotiation, delaying, and outright defiance are skills you must adapt when setting and enforcing bedtime rules. No matter what your child may throw at you at this age, you are the parent and the maker of rules. Beware of the hazards of over-scheduling, and always act in the firm belief that you do what you do to make sure your child gets enough sleep and learns the valuable behavioral skills he or she needs.

CHAPTER 9

Middle School and Beyond

By the time children reach middle school, many parents and certainly most, if not all, children believe that youngsters should more or less be on "automatic pilot" when

> *'I'm Not Tired Yet, and You're Not the Boss of Me'*

it comes to bedtime. But what does "automatic pilot" actually mean? It means, in fact, that there is no human pilot in control, and anything (or anyone) that is on automatic pilot for too long is prone to certain disaster. At some point, humans have to intervene to ensure that whatever or whoever is on automatic pilot is guided away from obstacles, slows to a stop where appropriate, and gets to its ultimate destination. The same is true for children and bedtimes. For those children who are placed on automatic pilot and end up deciding their own bedtime, parents are the human interveners. Of course, older youngsters (teens) should have more of a say on issues like bedtime than they did when they were much younger. But leaving the entire decision in their hands is sort of like handing a delicate object to an anvil salesman. In other words, bedtime and all that is associated with it (helpful rest, structure, regular routines) is too delicate, too fragile, and too important to be totally entrusted to a person whose idea of high humor is a knock-knock joke, and whose most cherished form of transportation is a skateboard. Let me say all this much more simply and straight-forwardly: You should set and enforce bedtimes for your children, even when those children are in middle school or well into high school.

Why? The biggest reason is that middle school-aged and high school-aged children do not often place rest high on their list of priorities. True, if left to their own devices, they would probably get enough sleep to be able to function for a week or maybe even two. But most likely they would quickly be using the weekends to catch up on lost sleep. It is not unusual for children who have late or no bedtimes during the week to sleep until even mid-afternoon on the weekends.

Another reason why parents should set and enforce reasonable bedtimes is that it creates a very powerful motivator for children, something we discussed earlier in the book. Specifically, if you set a strict bedtime – say, 8 p.m. for your middle school child or 9 p.m. for your high school child – but could live with a bedtime that's somewhat later (say, 9 or 9:30 p.m. for a middle schooler or 10:30 or 11 p.m. for a high schooler), you have created a powerful motivational tool virtually out of thin air. How? Research on child behavior shows that restricting events, activities, and commodities for children dramatically increases the value of those events, activities, and commodities. For example, embargoing your child's bike as a consequence for negative behavior increases the child's desire to ride it. Taking away the PlayStation 2 for a while increases a child's desire to play it. Forbidding your high school-aged daughter to hang out with a peer who you think is bad news increases the value your daughter places on hanging out with that peer. When you set an early bedtime and strictly stick to it, you dramatically increase the value of that hour past bedtime that your child could use to stay up later. As in our earlier example, setting a bedtime of 8 or 8:30 for a middle schooler, but being okay with a later bedtime of 9 or 9:30, creates roughly an hour of time that the child truly cherishes and desires. As an enterprising parent, you can then divide that extra hour (of temporal gold) into 15- or 30-minute blocks and use them to reward appropriate behavior. This tool works because the blocks of time have value to kids. And they don't cost you a cent, won't clutter up the house and need to be picked up later, and won't make you feel like you are in some way spoiling or overindulging your child through conspicuous consumption.

The beautiful part of this approach is that it can be used to motivate many types of behavior you would like to see. Let me share an example of how you can put this arrangement to work. Let's say you are having a difficult time getting your middle school daughter to do homework. First, you would tell your child that she is required to spend a certain amount of time – one hour – on homework each night. Also, she must complete the homework by 8 p.m. If the homework is not done by 8 p.m., you send her to bed with little fanfare and not much fun. You also tell her that you will wake her up one hour earlier than normal in the morning so that she can finish her homework.

If she spends the necessary minimum of an hour on homework and finishes by 8 p.m., she can stay up until 9 p.m. If she does an extra good job, meaning that she doesn't ask you for much help or she shows her appreciation for any help you provide (any parent who is willing to tackle middle school math, English, or science on his or her free time deserves at least a hug and "Thank you"), then she can stay up a bit longer, until 9:15.

Another advantage to this approach is the natural structure it imposes upon your child's day. Children who have clearly set expectations, consistency in their schedules, and routine requirements (chores), all established by or flowing from their parents, have much greater access to happiness than children who are left to their own devices. The simple fact is that the vast majority of children of middle school and high school age are still not quite capable of creating happiness for themselves, although most of them would certainly like to be given a blank check to try to do so. It is much easier for them to achieve happiness or other positive emotions when they have met expectations, fulfilled obligations, and shaped their own behavior so it fits with a consistent schedule. They may complain in the short term (they almost always do), but in the long term they will be genuinely healthier, happier, and better behaved. And this all ties very nicely into the value of ensuring that children get a proper amount of rest. No matter how old your children are – grade schoolers, middle schoolers, or high schoolers – they still need a lot of sleep.

So what is an appropriate bedtime for your older child? For your convenience, here is Richard Ferber's sleep chart again. Just find how many hours of sleep your child should get at his or her age and count backwards by that many hours from the time he or she must get up in the morning. That should give you your starting place for a bedtime. Then you can determine how much later of a bedtime you're comfortable with and use that cushion as your "motivation time."

Obviously, bedtimes might have some flexibility depending on things like whether it's the school year or summer, whether your child is involved in extracurricular school activities or other activities (church youth groups, choir, Boy

Typical Sleep Requirements in Childhood

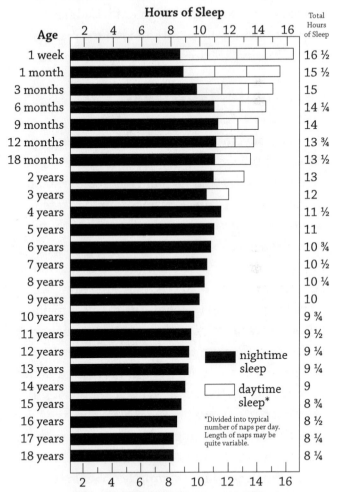

Reprinted with the permission of Simon & Schuster Adult Publishing Group
from HOW TO SOLVE YOUR CHILD'S SLEEP PROBLEMS by Richard Ferber,
M.D. Copyright © 1985 by Richard Ferber, M.D.

Scouts or Girls Scouts, etc.), and whether he or she
has a job. Use your best judgment based on the
premise that a well-rested child is a happier child,
which, in turn, will make you a happier parent.

Setting Up Bedtimes
for Older Children

Generally, the same types of strategies we've
discussed throughout this book, used in a slightly
more sophisticated way, could be used to establish
bedtimes and bedtime routines for older kids.
There are, however, some simple rules of thumb.
One is that the less talk about why a bedtime
has been set, the better. Please note that when
children use "Why?" to question a parental decision, they are usually not asking for a compelling
rationale. What they really want is information
with which they can take issue in an attempt to
undermine the authority of a parent's argument.
In other words, the word "Why'" coming out of a
child's mouth, especially when facing bedtime, is
an invitation to a bullfight. There are two problems with this: 1) It's not always clear who gets to
be the bull, and 2) It is distinctly possible that an
abundant amount of what comes out of one end

of the bull will be widely distributed during the fight. So the bottom line is that you should have some good reasons for setting a bedtime, tell your child what those reasons are, set the bedtime, and enforce it.

Another rule is to limit the extent to which extracurricular activities, homework, and undone chores interfere with the enforcement of a strict bedtime. Children have an uncanny ability to push their bedtimes to a later hour by suddenly remembering a lot of things they just have to do right before it's time for bed. One way to handle this is to have children go to bed on time, then wake them earlier than usual to complete whatever chores or activities they didn't finish the night before. Over time, children will realize that getting up before the newspaper delivery person (unless they are newspaper deliverers) is not much fun, and they will start taking care of their evening activities more productively.

A final rule is to limit the amount of electronic stimulation that is available to your child in his or her bedroom after bedtime. A little reading (15 to 30 minutes) is probably okay. But high-intensity video games, chain saw rock n' roll music played at outdoor concert levels, instant messaging, GameBoying, X-2-ing, PS-2-ing, and all other such stimulating activities are inconsistent with the reduced arousal level necessary for a smooth transition to sleep. In short, when it's bedtime, these activities should be history.

Summary

A final word on children in middle school and beyond. This is advice as well as a warning. Ensuring that children at these ages get the required rest is a very important, helpful, and loving thing for a parent to do. Sadly, as Shakespeare once said, "There is no fang sharper than an ungrateful child." You are likely to be harangued, possibly despised, certainly dismissed, and probably made the object of scorn for doing the right thing. Any parent who expects gratitude for doing the right thing is going to be sorely disappointed. But do it anyway.

CHAPTER 10

Special Sleep Issues

There is a range of special issues that pertain to bedtime and child sleep problems that are worthy of mention. They are not sufficiently tied to what has been discussed thus far, so I will comment on each of them briefly. I also recommend that if any of these become an abiding concern, you should consult with your primary care physician about each one.

Bed-Wetting

At the age of 6 years, approximately 15 percent of girls and 25 percent of boys are still wetting the bed. This is a social and developmental concern, and possibly a medical concern. A medical concern can be ruled out easily with a simple physical conducted by your primary care physician. If medical problems are ruled out (and they are in about 95 percent of cases), then we are left with developmental and social issues, and the bed-wetting child is the ultimate person to determine how much these should concern us. Treatments that are touted as cures or systematic relief are available, and physicians or well-trained psychologists can prescribe them. If that is of interest to parents or the child or both, I recommend consulting the primary care physician first.

However, I can give advice here that should absolutely be followed even before another professional is contacted: Children should never be punished for nocturnal incontinence. The chances that a child is wetting the bed on purpose are so small that it shouldn't even be considered. Rather, it is a virtual certainty that the problem is entirely out of the child's control, and children should never be punished for anything that is entirely out of their control.

Nightmares

At one time or another, all children will have nightmares, as will adults. And uniformly, across the age span, nightmares are distressing to the people who have them. When a child has a nightmare, it is best to provide just enough parental soothing and concern to calm him or her down and to encourage the child to go back to sleep. Nothing reduces the power of a nightmare better than falling back to sleep and gaining distance from it. Whether your young child should be allowed to sleep with you after a nightmare is an open question. If you can guarantee yourself and your child that this solution will occur only for one night, then it's no problem. If it is the dawn of a new habit, however, other problems are likely to emerge. You may want to think of allowing your child to sleep in your bed after a nightmare as a powerful habit-forming substance for the child. There are a lot of powerful habit-forming substances that adults sometimes seek and need. The fact that these substances are habit forming doesn't mean they shouldn't be used; it just means they should be used cautiously and in small amounts. When considering whether to let a child sleep in an adult bed because the child is having nightmares, my advice is to consider strongly how necessary it is. If you decide it is necessary, do so in small amounts and only for a limited period.

Night Terrors and Sleepwalking

Night terrors are not nightmares. Nightmares are events that children are aware of as they occur and can remember long after they are over. Night terrors are dramatically different in both respects. When children have night terrors, they are entirely unaware they are occurring, so there is nothing for them to remember. Night terrors occur at the deepest stages of sleep, and in that stage no awareness is possible. Unfortunately for parents and other persons in the house, when children have night terrors, anyone within a wide geographical range is aware they are occurring and will remember them long afterwards. In other words, a night terror is often terrifying for everyone except the child who is having one. Similarly, sleepwalking also occurs in the deepest stage of sleep, a stage where no awareness or memory is possible. Thus, it is not necessary to wake a child who is having a night terror or who is sleepwalking. It is, however, absolutely critical to ensure their safety. During a night terror, children may become extremely agitated or will scream loudly. They are at risk of falling out of the bed, and parents must ensure that doesn't happen. The event also may affect other children in the household, and parents should direct some of their attention to them. As I said, it isn't necessary to wake a child who is having a night terror; in fact, doing so may actually distress the child beyond what is necessary. That is, while having the night terror, they are entirely unconscious, but when they are awakened, they are in the presence of concerned, and possibly distraught, adults. This could be upsetting to children.

Similarly, children who are sleepwalking are at risk for obvious reasons. These children should be redirected to their room and put back in bed. Then some safeguards should be put into place so that they cannot leave again. When either of these sleep events occur, it is best to consult with the primary care physician.

Storms, Things That Go Bump in the Night

Things that happen in the night are scarier than things that happen in the day. Storms are scary enough in the day but they are very scary at night. Many things that go bump in the day are frightening but they are a thousand times more so at night. When children are experiencing either of these, they are likely to become distressed and will need to be soothed. My general advice, provided earlier, is to supply just enough support and concern to calm your child down so he or she can go back to sleep. If it is necessary for the child to come into your bed for that to happen, that's okay. But it is important to remember that you are then supplying that powerful habit-forming substance I mentioned earlier. As I've said, such substances should be supplied in small amounts and only for a limited time.

Illness

Sleep needs for children who are ill are different from sleep needs for children who are well. My general recommendation for children who are ill is to obtain the primary care physician's recommendations about how to manage their sleep.

CHAPTER 11

Wrapping It Up

Well, it is time to put this book to bed, so to speak. The commitment of the book is to supply beleaguered parents, whose beloved children don't have the critical bedtime knowledge and skills (particularly in the areas involving when to go to bed, how long to stay, and what to do when there), with practical solutions. Early on I explained the difference between sleep problems – bedtime difficulties that involve the lack of knowledge and skills just mentioned – and sleep disorders – difficulties that even well-intentioned parents and highly willing children are not able to solve without professional assistance. I want to reiterate here that if you are concerned or are unsure about whether your child's bedtime difficulty is a sleep problem or a sleep disorder, you should seek professional assistance.

Another key message well worth repeating is that the bedrock, cornerstone, foundation, basis, or ontological predicate (that one was for you crossword puzzlers) of any parental attempt to solve bedtime problems is the pre-bedtime ritual. It is during this ritual that parents supply the love children need in order to successfully make the solo journey from "Good night, sleep tight" to "Good morning, how nice to see you." All of the bedtime strategies I have described are second to this ritual. It precedes the longest period of time children spend alone during their day, and it allows the best of what parents have to offer their kids – their love – to stay with the children during that time. (Just thinking about it now makes me want to either get a hug or reach for a teddy bear.)

A final critical point involves the relationship between bedtime practices used by parents, bedtime behaviors exhibited by children, and the learning process. Children are always learning, and experience is their most powerful teacher. Experiences that occur at night are particularly powerful because of the potent effect fatigue and darkness have on how children feel. Well-meaning parents who are unaware of learning processes can easily teach their children ineffective ways to manage fatigue and darkness. Knowledge of learning processes, however, enables parents to harness those processes and successfully teach their children critical bedtime skills.

Whether your child is an infant, a toddler, a preschooler, or an elementary school, middle school, or high school student (or a combination thereof), I wish you all the best as you try some new ways to send him or her off (on time) to a sleep of sweet dreams and needed rest. Good night.

ABOUT THE AUTHOR

Dr. Patrick Friman, Ph.D., is the Director of the Outpatient Behavioral Pediatric and Family Services Clinic at Boys Town, a Clinical Professor of Pediatrics at the University of Nebraska School of Medicine, and the editor of the *Journal of Applied Behavior Analysis*. He is the author of more than 140 published scientific papers on child behavior topics, and he has also held faculty appointments at the Johns Hopkins University School of Medicine, the University of Pennsylvania School of Medicine, and the University of Nevada.

A central theme of Dr. Friman's work over the past 20 years has been the discovery and distribution of knowledge about children that is practical, readily understood, and useful. This book is a product of some of that work.

Kid-friendly books to teach social skills

Reinforce the social skills RJ learns in each book by ordering its corresponding teacher's activity guide and skill posters by Julia Cook.

978-1-934490-20-4
978-1-934490-34-1 (SPANISH)
978-1-934490-23-5 (ACTIVITY GUIDE)

978-1-934490-25-9
978-1-934490-53-2 (SPANISH)
978-1-934490-27-3 (ACTIVITY GUIDE)

978-1-934490-28-0
978-1-934490-32-7 (ACTIVITY GUIDE)

978-1-934490-35-8
978-1-934490-37-2 (ACTIVITY GUIDE)

978-1-934490-43-3
978-1-934490-45-7 (ACTIVITY GUIDE)

978-1-934490-49-5
978-1-934490-51-8 (ACTIVITY GUIDE)

978-1-934490-67-9
978-1-934490-69-3 (ACTIVITY GUIDE)

Help kids get along.

 Building RELATIONSHIPS

Help kids master the art of communicating.

COMMUNICATE with **Confidence**

Help kids take responsibility for their behavior.

978-1-934490-97-6

978-1-934490-86-0

Other Titles: Making Friends Is an Art!, Cliques Just Don't Make Cents, Tease Monster, Peer Pressure Gauge, Hygiene... You Stink!

978-1-934490-76-1

978-1-934490-58-7

Other Title: Well, I Can Top That!

978-1-934490-90-7

978-1-934490-80-8

Other Title: But It's Not My Fault

978-1-934490-85-3

978-1-934490-96-9

978-1-934490-74-7

Titles from Bryan Smith

 WILLIE BOHANON URBAN CHARACTER EDUCATION

Titles from Kip Jones
Other Title: The Power of Self-D

Titles from Stephie McCumbie

Other Title: Priscilla & the Perfect Storm

978-1-934490-87-7

978-1-934490-54-9

978-1-934490-77-8

978-1-934490-79-2

978-1-934490-92-1

BOYS TOWN Press

BoysTownPress.org

For information on Boys Town, its Education Model®, Common Sense Parenting®, and training programs:
boystowntraining.org | boystown.org/parenting
training@BoysTown.org | 1-800-545-5771

For parenting and educational books and other resources:
BoysTownPress.org
btpress@BoysTown.org
1-800-282-6657